I0816276

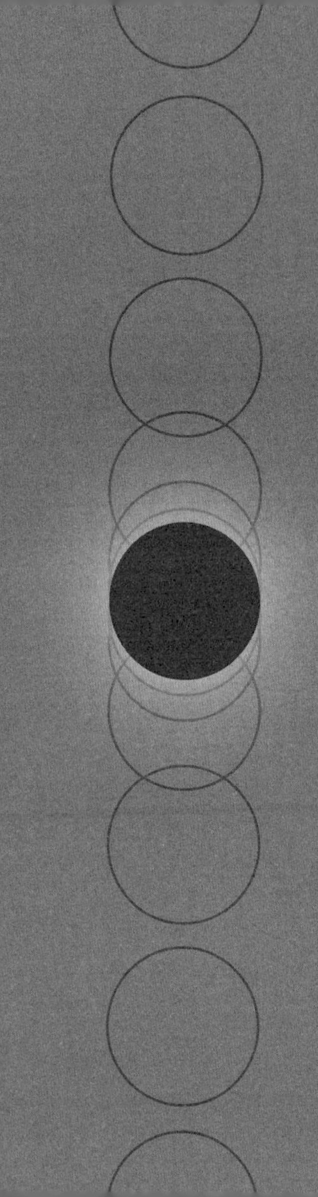

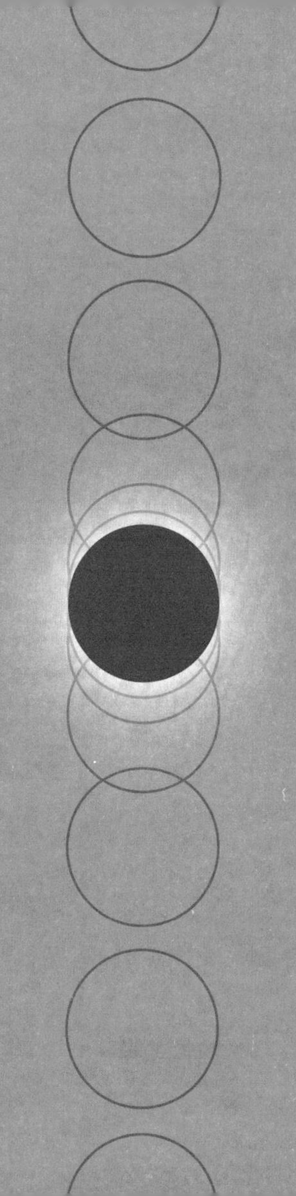

LLEWELLYN'S
Little Book of
# PENDULUMS

Richard Webster (New Zealand) is the bestselling author of more than one hundred books. Richard has appeared on several radio and television programs in the US and abroad, including guest spots on WMAQ-TV (Chicago), KTLA-TV (Los Angeles), and KSTW-TV (Seattle). He travels regularly, lecturing and conducting workshops on a variety of metaphysical subjects. His bestselling titles include *Spirit Guides & Angel Guardians* and *Creative Visualization for Beginners*. Learn more at Psychic.co.nz.

LLEWELLYN'S

Little Book of

# PENDULUMS

RICHARD WEBSTER

FIRST EDITION
First Printing, 2026

Cover cartouche by Freepik
Cover design by Shira Atakpu
Interior art by Llewellyn Art Department



Library of Congress Cataloging-in-Publication Data Pending
ISBN: 978-0-7387-7898-3



Llewellyn Publications
A Division of Llewellyn Worldwide Ltd.
2143 Wooddale Drive
Woodbury, MN 55125-2989
www.llewellyn.com

Printed in China

GPSR Representation:
UPI-2M PLUS d.o.o., Medulićeva 20, 10000 Zagreb, Croatia
matt.parsons@upi2mbooks.hr

For my lifelong friend, Robyn Berry Luke,
who loves pendulums as much as I do

# Contents

# Exercises

# Introduction

Wouldn't it be wonderful to have a device that can provide answers to your questions, find lost objects, help you make good decisions, develop your intuition, and assist you in many other ways? Amazingly, the small dowsing tool called a pendulum can enable you to do these things and more.

"Dowsing" is the term used to describe the act of divining (searching) for anything the person desires using their body or by holding a forked stick, L-shaped metal rods, or a pendulum. When the person is close to whatever they are searching for, the instrument reacts. Most people have heard of dowsers locating underground water (usually with a forked stick), but in addition to finding water, dowsing is regularly used to find lost objects, animals, and people, as well as precious objects such as gold, silver, diamonds, and other minerals. Dowsing can also be used to detect impurities in food, answer questions, divine the future, eliminate negativity, enhance spiritual growth, and aid spiritual healing.

This book focuses on dowsing with a pendulum and consequently doesn't discuss other dowsing devices such as rods or sticks. This is because the pendulum is arguably the easiest dowsing device to use, as it is simply a small weight known as a "bob," suspended on a length of string or chain. Ideally, the bob should weigh at least a few ounces, though when nothing else was available, I've had to use paper clips and other light weights, including a Christmas tree decoration. They all worked well. My mother used her wedding ring attached to a length of thread and it always worked well for her. Consequently, the bob can be almost anything but should not be so heavy that your hand and arm get tired when using it.

As for the bob, almost anything that can be suspended on a length of thread, string, or chain works. Because of my interest in pendulums, friends and family members have given me a wide variety of items over the years ranging from a small plastic skull to a miniature New Testament. I enjoy experimenting with every unusual pendulum I've been given but have yet to find one I'd consider using for serious dowsing experiments.

A friend of mine suffers from a variety of allergies and uses her pendulum to test the meals she orders in restaurants to determine if they are safe for her to eat. I know people who use their pendulums to communicate with animals and have even met someone who wrote a book using a pendulum. It's amazing how useful this simple device can be.

By the time you've finished reading this book, you'll know how to use a pendulum to find almost anything hidden, such as underground water. You'll have learned how to dowse for anything that's lost, improve your health, learn about your past lives and future trends, and even how to develop spiritually.

All successful dowsers know that the pendulum provides them with answers, and that's all they care about. The purpose of this book is to help you become a successful dowser.

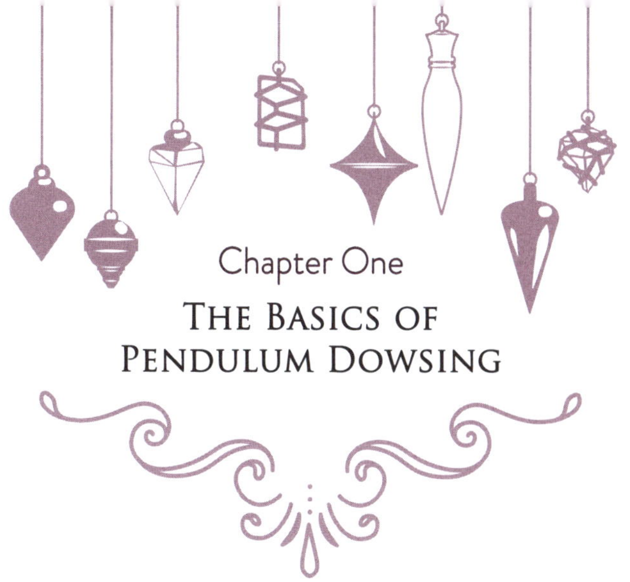

# Chapter One
# The Basics of Pendulum Dowsing

In his history of the Roman Empire, Ammianus Marcellinus (ca. 325–391 CE) recorded what may have been the first written mention of a pendulum. He wrote that in the first century CE, a group of people were arrested for plotting to kill the emperor. In his confession, one of the conspirators told of a priest who held a ring suspended on a thread over a circular platter that had the letters of the alphabet engraved around the rim. The ring moved and indicated the letters *T*, *H*, *E*, and *O*. This told the conspirators that the next emperor would be Theodorus.

In 1830, Michel-Eugène Chevreul, the director of the Natural History Museum in Paris, became interested in the pendulum and concluded that the unconscious will of the person holding it created the pendulum's movements. These involuntary movements are described as the ideomotor response. However, it is not yet known what causes the hand to move when the pendulum has located the object it is searching for.

It's possible to influence the movements of a pendulum with your thoughts. If you hold a pendulum and will it to move in a clockwise circle, it will do exactly that. You can then ask it to move in a different direction, such as from side to side, and it will change to reflect whatever direction your mind is concentrating on.

Because your mind is able to make this happen, it's probably not surprising that your pendulum can also answer questions by tapping into the universal mind. Your conscious mind enables you to function in the everyday world of facts and anything that can be proven. Your subconscious mind ensures that you breathe and your heart keeps beating. You don't have to consciously think about doing these things. Your subconscious mind also acts as a storehouse containing memories of everything you've ever experienced. Your subconscious mind is able to access the universal mind that has knowledge of everything. That is why you can go to bed at night with an apparently unsolvable problem and wake up in the morning with the solution. Your mind has incredible power that is able to give you any information you may require.

When you're using a pendulum to find something, you obviously have no idea where it is, but the universal mind that knows everything does. Consequently, if you dowse with a sense of confident expectation, your subconscious mind will receive the information from the universal mind, and your pendulum will respond and give you the answer.

Many dowsers believe that everything vibrates in a particular, individual way, and it is these vibrations that are being picked up subconsciously by the dowser and revealed by the pendulum.

Another possibility is that dowsers are using their clairvoyant skills to find whatever is hidden and cause the pendulum to react. The word "clairvoyance" means knowing what is not known, and that is exactly what a pendulum does.

People do better at dowsing when they're willing to suspend disbelief. If you're prepared to be open-minded and let the pendulum do the work your dowsing skills will grow rapidly.

Dr. Zaboj V. Harvalik, a Czechoslovakian physicist who taught at the University of Missouri, conducted an extensive series of tests on dowsing in the 1960s. One of his findings was that people who appeared to have no dowsing ability would discover they actually could dowse successfully after drinking half a glass of whiskey. The alcohol relaxed them enough to suspend their disbelief and enabled them to become efficient dowsers (Wilson 1988, 116).

## How to Choose a Pendulum

You can buy pendulums at metaphysical stores, psychic fairs, crystal stores, at many gift stores, and online. Many people like the convenience of buying a pendulum online. Of course, depending on where you live, this might be the only way you can obtain a pendulum. Whenever possible, though, I like to hold and test a pendulum before purchasing it to find out how it responds to me.

When choosing a pendulum, you may find a pendulum that seems to talk to you when you're holding it. Silently ask it if it wants you to look after it. You'll receive a response in your body. It's likely to be subtle, such as a tingling feeling. It may be a sense that the pendulum is responding to your question. When that happens, your search is over—you should buy that particular pendulum.

You may find your intuition tells you to buy a particular pendulum sometimes even before you pick it up. There's no need to worry if you don't feel anything at all when examining a selection of pendulums. Everyone is different, and we all respond in different ways. Simply choose the pendulum that feels right and is most aesthetically appealing to you.

The best pendulum for you is one that looks attractive and responds quickly and easily. The pendulum should not be too heavy or light: A light one will make small movements that might be hard to discern, and a heavy pendulum can become tiring to hold after a while. A good weight for most people is approximately three ounces. Symmetrical, spherical, and cylindrical shapes (especially ones that have a point at the bottom) all work well.

Some pendulums contain a hollow compartment inside them. These pendulums usually have a screw top with a small compartment inside the weight. This enables the dowser to place a small sample of whatever it is the dowser is searching for inside the compartment before using it. If you're searching for water, for instance, you could place a few drops of water into the compartment.

If you're looking for gold, you'd place a small piece of gold into the compartment. You could place a hair from a missing pet inside the compartment if they are lost. You can even write a small message on a piece of paper explaining what you're searching for and place that inside the compartment.

Pendulums that contain a compartment are usually called witness pendulums. Some people call them sample or hollow chamber pendulums. Witness pendulums are believed to have been invented by Abbé Mermet, an early twentieth-century French priest who had an international reputation for his skill with the pendulum. You can still buy Mermet pendulums today. They are made of a brass alloy and contain a compartment inside that can contain a sample of whatever the dowser is divining for.

The material the pendulum is made from is important, too. Pendulums made from wood, glass, crystal, plastic, and metal are all available in stores. Crystal pendulums are always popular. As well as looking attractive, crystals also receive, hold, and transmit energy. All crystals work well, but some crystals are more popular than others due to the attributes they possess. Rose quartz, for instance, relates to peace, love, and the heart; amethyst relates to spirituality, protection, and healing; blue lace agate provides energy and stimulates the mind. Clear quartz vibrates at a high frequency and cleanses the soul. It also provides clarity and can be used for any purpose.

## How to Make a Pendulum

Not long ago, it wasn't easy to buy pendulums; most people had to make their own. Many people, my mother included, used their wedding ring and a length of thread. A major advantage of making your own pendulum is that you'll fill it with your energy in the process of making it.

Almost anything that can be attached to a length of string can be used to make a pendulum. A fishing sinker, a large button, a nut, seashell, or a small ornament can all be used as weights to make effective pendulums. At different times when nothing else was available, I've used my car keys, a tea bag, a curtain cord, needle and thread, a Christmas tree decoration, an apple core, and even dental floss using the container it came in as the weight as impromptu pendulums. An elderly dowser I know uses a gold fob watch and chain as his pendulum.

A simple pendulum can be made by threading one or more beads to several inches of cord. A necklace or a pendant work well as pendulums. For some years, I used a pendulum made from an old key I bought from an antique shop. I attached it to a chain and wore it around my neck so that I had a pendulum with me all the time.

You can make an attractive pendulum by wrapping a crystal or gemstone with string, cord, or beading thread. Two twelve-inch lengths of wire can be twisted together to contain a crystal or gemstone. Hold the pieces of wire together and make three twists in the center. Bend the pieces of wire at the bottom to create a V to serve as the base so your crystal can rest in it. Make three more twists to match the first three you made. Separate the two wires and run them around the crystal to help contain it and then continue twisting and separating the wires until you reach the top of the crystal. Make sure that the wires are kept as close to the stone as possible. Form a loop at the top of the crystal and then trim any excess wire. Thread or loop a length of thread or string to complete the pendulum.

You can also make attractive pendulums from dry, straight twigs or small branches of trees. I like to use willow twigs that have fallen from the tree.

Start by sandpapering the twig to remove the bark and make the pendulum weight smooth to the touch. Using a file, create a point at one end of the twig. Attach an eye screw to the other end and finish by attaching a length of thread or cord to it. If you wish, you can decorate the finished weight with a woodburning pen or colored markers.

## How to Cleanse Your Pendulum

Before using any pendulum, it must be cleansed. Like everything else, your pendulum picks up positive, neutral, and negative energy. If you've bought your pendulum online or from a store, it will have picked up a great deal of energy before reaching you. Hopefully that energy is all positive, but chances are there'll be plenty of negative energy attached to it as well—plenty of people will have handled it from the time it was made to when it reaches you, after all. Any one of those people may have been upset or in a bad mood while handling it, and that negativity will now be attached to your beautiful new pendulum.

There are a number of ways to remove any negative energy before using a pendulum. Obviously, your intention with any method is to cleanse your pendulum, and to restore it to a pristine condition, so keep this thought in mind while doing the cleansing.

### Smoke Cleansing

You can burn aromatic herbs such as sage, lavender, and rosemary, and then hold your pendulum over the smoke.

The most convenient way to do this is to purchase burning herb bundles from New Age stores and online. Most people think of sage with these bundles, but there are many other options, all of which work well. I prefer to do this kind of cleansing outdoors and always have a large container of water with me, just in case any embers from the herb cause a fire. I also have a large glass casserole dish to drop the smudge stick into if necessary—always treat fire with great care.

### Earth

If your pendulum is rustproof, you can bury it in soil for at least twenty-four hours. I use a sunny part of my garden for this. You can also bury it in the soil of a potted plant.

### Salt

Salt has been used for purification and cleansing for thousands of years. All you need to do is to rest your pendulum on top of a small bowl of pure salt and leave it there overnight. Some people prefer to bury the pendulum in the salt but it's not essential.

### Quartz

If you keep your pendulum in a small bag, you can tuck in a small piece of clear quartz with it overnight to cleanse your crystal.

### Breath

A quick and useful way to purify your pendulum is to rest your pendulum in your cupped hands and to blow over it while thinking of your intention. Change the position of your pendulum between breaths to make sure that every part of it receives your breath. If you use your pendulum with clients, this is a quick and effective way to cleanse it between appointments.

### Moonlight

You can also cleanse your pendulum by resting it for a few hours in moonlight or sunlight. I like to place my pendulums on a windowsill overnight to enable them to be cleansed by the energy of the moon shining on them. You can also cleanse them with sunlight. Be aware that some crystals fade in sunlight, so make sure you don't leave them exposed to the sun's rays for extended periods of time.

# Effective Crystals for Pendulums

Although you can use any crystal you wish as your pendulum bob, crystals produce a variety of types of energy that can be harnessed when you're divining for a particular purpose. Here are some of the most popular crystals that are used for their particular energies:

- Clear quartz for healing, energy, and positive intentions
- Amethyst for spirituality and protection
- Rose quartz for love, harmony, compassion, and decision making
- Black tourmaline for grounding, protection, and guidance
- Citrine for guidance and abundance
- Labradorite for wisdom, courage, and peace of mind
- Carnelian for confidence, self-esteem, and truth
- Sodalite for communication, mindfulness, and peace
- Aventurine for positivity and good fortune
- Fluorite for thoughtfulness, clarity, and clear thinking

## How to Use a Pendulum

Now that your pendulum has been cleansed, it's time to start using it. It's best to practice on your own until you feel comfortable with your pendulum. You don't want anyone with you who is skeptical or tries to ridicule what you're doing. Choose a quiet, comfortable space where you can practice in peace. You need to feel positive and confident that you'll quickly master the art and become a good pendulum dowser.

Sit down at a table with the chain or cord of your pendulum held between the thumb and first finger of your dominant hand (your right hand if you're right-handed, your left hand if you're left-handed). Rest the elbow of the arm holding the pendulum on the table. Your legs should be uncrossed, feet flat on the floor. The palm of the hand holding the pendulum should be slightly curved and facing downward with the bob of the pendulum hanging approximately seven to twelve inches in front of you.

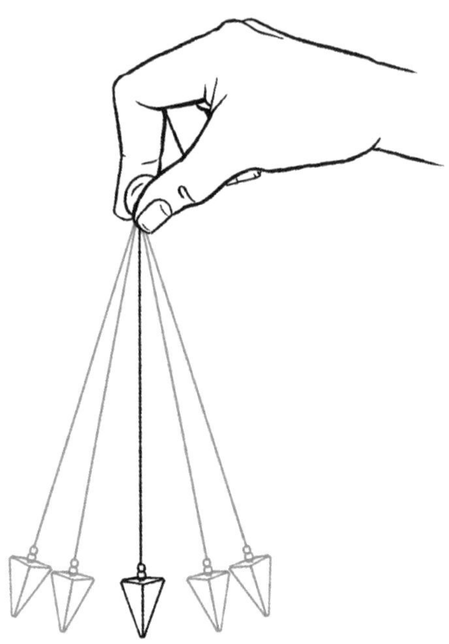

Figure 1: *How to Hold a Pendulum*

Start by swinging the pendulum gently in circles in both clockwise and counterclockwise directions. Once you've done this, swing the pendulum from side to side, and then forward (away from you) and backward (toward you). You can also swing your pendulum diagonally. The purpose of doing this is to become familiar with the different movements your pendulum can make.

You can also experiment by holding the cord or chain at different lengths to see what length works best for you. Four to five inches seems to be about right for most people, but you may prefer a shorter or longer length than that. A good way to test different lengths is to allow the cord to slip slowly between your thumb and first finger until the bob swings easily in all directions.

After trying motions with your dominant hand, try swinging the pendulum in your nondominant hand. Most people prefer using their dominant hand with a pendulum, but you may find it easier to use your other hand.

While you're getting used to your pendulum, try hanging it over the first joint of your index finger with your thumb holding the cord in position. I've met many dowsers who prefer holding their pendulums this way, and you may find that this position feels more comfortable than pinching it between your thumb and first finger. The only disadvantage of holding your pendulum this way is that you need to look at the bob of the pendulum to see what movement it's making. When held between the thumb and first finger, you can tell (with practice) what motion the pendulum is making without constantly looking at it.

Spend as long as you wish familiarizing yourself with the different movements your pendulum can make. When you feel ready to progress further, put your pendulum down for a few minutes and drink some water. It's important to be well hydrated before dowsing.

## How to Start Working with Your Pendulum

With practice, you'll find you'll be able to use your pendulum anywhere. However, you'll find it easier initially to start your experiments while sitting at a table, with your feet flat on the floor, and the elbow of the arm that's going to hold the pendulum resting on the table. Make yourself comfortable and take a few slow, deep breaths to help release any tension in your body.

When you feel calm and relaxed, pick up your pendulum, hold it between your thumb and first finger in a relaxed grip, and use your free hand to stop the movements of the bob. When it's still, ask your pendulum which movement indicates a "yes" or positive response. You can communicate with your pendulum silently or out loud. If you're fortunate, your pendulum might immediately start moving and indicate a positive response. It's more likely that your pendulum will move slightly, or maybe not move at all. Be patient and keep asking your pendulum to indicate its positive response. Again: stop after five minutes if your pendulum fails to move and try again later. If nothing happens after five minutes, put your pendulum down and try again later.

Without exception, everyone can learn to use a pendulum. There's no need to worry if it takes longer than you thought it would to be able to use it. If you practice for five minutes a day, it won't take long until your pendulum starts responding. The problem may simply be that you're trying too hard. In this case, you're likely to be feeling tense and are approaching your pendulum with grim determination. The remedy for this is to relax as much as you can before picking up your pendulum and asking it to indicate your positive response.

There may be matters going on in your life that affect the movements of the pendulum. Your pendulum may refuse to work if you're angry, under major stress, overtired, have consumed too much alcohol, or are finding it hard to concentrate on what you're doing. External factors such as trying to use your pendulum for the first time in cramped or crowded conditions or with other people watching can also adversely affect your pendulum's movements.

Don't experiment with your pendulum when you're rushed and short on time—it will probably refuse to work. Your pendulum will answer quick questions once you're used to working with it, but it's best to allow your pendulum as much time as necessary to respond while you're learning. Once you've become used to working with it, you'll find responses will come as soon as you think of a question.

There are a number of things you can do if you continue to have problems. You may find it easier to start the pendulum's movements yourself. Swing your pendulum back and forth or from side to side. Once it's moving freely, ask it to move in circles. Don't help it to do this. Simply visualize and imagine it happening. Allow the pendulum to gyrate for several seconds and then think that you want it to move from side to side (or back and forth) again. Once the pendulum has followed your thoughts and acted on your request, ask it to gyrate again this time in a clockwise direction (if it moved counterclockwise the first time), or vice versa. Finally, stop the movement of your pendulum with your free hand and ask it to show its positive response.

Another suggestion is to stop asking your pendulum to indicate its positive response. Instead, focus your attention on the bob and visualize it moving from side to side. This generally works. Once the pendulum starts moving, you can then ask it to indicate your positive response. Your pendulum will not change direction if a side-to-side movement is your positive response. However, if it isn't, your pendulum will gradually move to indicate the correct response.

Another solution is to ask someone who is proficient with the pendulum to rest their hand on whatever shoulder of yours that belongs to the hand you are holding the pendulum with. Again, ask the pendulum to give a positive response, and you'll find the bob will start to move.

### • • • Exercise 1 • • •
### *The Battery Test*

This is a fascinating experiment that usually provides you with your pendulum's positive and negative responses.

1. Obtain an AA battery and place it on a table in front of you.
2. Suspend your pendulum over the top (positive) end of the battery. Your pendulum will start moving, usually indicating your pendulum's positive response.

3. Suspend your pendulum over the other (negative) end of the battery. This time your pendulum will swing or circle in a movement that usually indicates your negative response.
4. Suspend your pendulum over the center of the battery. The weight will start swinging to and fro, from one end to the other.

In almost every case, this experiment provides dowsers with their positive and negative responses. However, I've worked with a few people where this didn't happen, and the responses were different to their usual "yes" and "no" responses. If you haven't yet discovered your pendulum's responses, use this exercise as a way to start your pendulum moving. Once you've learned your responses, try this experiment again to see if those movements agree with those you observed with the battery.

The following is another practice sometimes used to help people start receiving positive and negative responses. Sit with your legs apart and your feet flat on the floor. Hold the pendulum over your right knee and close your eyes for about thirty seconds. When you open your eyes, your pendulum should be moving and will usually indicate your positive or yes response. Repeat this by holding your pendulum over your left knee. When you open your eyes, your pendulum will be moving in a different direction to the one it made over your right knee. This will usually indicate your negative or no response.

You can do a similar experiment using one of your hands. Hold the hand not using the pendulum palm down in front of you. Suspend the pendulum over the back of your hand and see what response it gives. With most people it will revolve in clockwise circles, generally a positive or "yes" motion. Now turn the hand over and hold your pendulum over the palm of your hand. This time your pendulum will probably revolve in counterclockwise circles, generally a negative or "no" response. Everyone is unique, however, so responses may differ.

Once your pendulum has given you your "yes" and "no" answers, ask it to indicate what responses indicate "I don't know" and "I don't want to answer."

The four directions your pendulum has given you will probably stay the same for the rest of your life. However, whenever you haven't used your pendulum for a while, it's a good idea to confirm that these directions are still the same and haven't changed.

## Your Pendulum Diary

It's difficult to evaluate your progress without keeping a record of your successes and failures. You can keep something as simple as a notebook as your pendulum diary, or you might like to keep the results as a file on your computer or phone. As well as recording your questions and your pendulum's responses, it's also important to record the outcomes of each experiment. It can be fascinating to look back over past entries and see how your accuracy and success rate improve the more you use your pendulum.

## Sacred Space

A sacred space is a quiet, safe, and private place where you can perform your ritualistic and spiritual practices. You can also use it as a special place to relax, meditate, and pray in. It's an especially good place for working with your pendulum. Depending on the weather where you live, you might choose to have your sacred space outdoors. That's not practical for everyone, and most people choose somewhere inside their home that is reasonably private. The area doesn't need to be large, especially if you'll be working on your own; a corner of a room is often all you need. Over a period of time, your sacred space will gain a powerful and positive energy that your more intuitive friends will sense when they visit your home.

Your pendulum will help you find the most suitable place in your home for your sacred space. Start by standing at your front door and ask your pendulum to indicate the direction of the best position in your home to set up a sacred space. Once you have the direction, you can move from room to room until your pendulum indicates the exact position.

You can put whatever you wish inside your sacred space. You'll probably need a table or at least a shelf to act as an altar to work on, and a chair. You'll also need some shelves or a cupboard to keep any supplies you might need, such as candles, incense, tarot cards, crystals, books, wands, and religious or spiritual objects. You might like to hang some art on the wall.

Before using your sacred space, remove any negative or stagnant energy that might be lingering in the area by sitting in the center of your sacred space and swinging your pendulum counterclockwise until it stops. This dissipates the negative energy. Follow this by swinging it in a clockwise direction to attract positive, beneficial energy.

Instead of doing this sitting down, you may prefer to walk around your sacred space while swinging your pendulum.

Once your pendulum is responding to your thoughts, you're ready to move onto the next stage and start asking it questions, covered in the next chapter.

# Chapter Two
# How to Ask Questions

You can ask your pendulum any question you wish. The only proviso is that it must be answerable with a "yes" or a "no." You can, for instance, ask your pendulum if it would be worth your while to attend a particular lecture, decide on which book to read, choose a pet, or name a baby.

Your questions need to have a purpose. This is called your intent. If you know exactly what you're asking for, you can frame your questions in the right way to answer them. Having an intent also stops you from asking frivolous questions.

Your pendulum will provide you with accurate answers to serious questions, but it will give frivolous answers, or possibly refuse to give an answer at all, to frivolous questions.

Once your pendulum has responded, don't ask the same question again. Even if the pendulum didn't give you the answer you wanted, asking the question again creates doubt in the veracity of the pendulum's answers, and your subconscious mind might overrule the pendulum and give you the answer you want to hear even though it might be incorrect.

## Protection

Before asking any questions, you need to protect yourself from any negative energies that might be attracted to your pendulum. Most of the time protection isn't necessary, but it's a good habit to get into, as then you won't forget to do it when dowsing for anything that could be negative or harmful, such as geopathic stress.

There are many ways to protect yourself. I usually stand with my legs slightly apart and my arms resting by my sides. I take three slow, deep breaths and visualize a pure white light descending from the universal life force (God, infinite spirit, Architect of the Universe, or whatever name you choose) over me. Imagine the white light filling your body with protective energy and then overflowing to surround you with a large bubble of protection.

An alternative method is to consciously expand your aura. Your aura is the electromagnetic field that completely surrounds your body. It is shaped like a large egg and extends eight to ten feet from your physical body. You can expand the size of your aura by taking slow, deep breaths. Visualize yourself breathing in each of the colors of the rainbow (red, orange, yellow, green, blue, indigo, and violet), one at a time, and imagine the colors spreading to every cell of your body before radiating out into your aura, strengthening and enlarging it with every breath.

## Can I, May I, Should I?

It's important to get permission from your higher self before doing any serious work with your pendulum. You might, for instance, ask: "Is it in the best interests of everyone concerned with this matter for me to dowse today for (whatever it happens to be)?"

# How to Create Effective Questions

Your success depends upon asking clear and specific questions. Here are some suggestions on how to do that.

Always start with "Can I?", "May I?", and "Should I?" questions.

Once you've done that, ask questions that can be answered with a yes or no response.

Be specific. Include names, times, places, and any other details that will make your question as effective as possible. Vague questions receive vague answers.

Ask positive questions. It's better to ask: "Will I have an enjoyable vacation in Vermont?" than, "Will my vacation in Vermont be difficult?

Ask simple questions. It's better to ask a few simple questions that follow on from each other than one complicated question containing a number of variables.

If you have an emotional involvement in the answer, ask someone who has no connection with the outcome to hold the pendulum for you.

You might prefer to ask your pendulum three questions before starting to dowse: "Can I?", "May I?", and "Should I?"

"Can I?" asks the Universal Life Force if you possess the necessary skills to successfully dowse for whatever it is you are searching for.

"May I?" confirms that you have permission from everyone involved in the outcome. If you're dowsing a house to find something that's been lost, for instance, this means that you have the necessary permission from the owner of the house as well as the owner of the lost object.

"Should I?" confirms that what you're planning to do is in the best interests of everyone concerned. It also ensures that you're in the right state of mind to perform the dowsing, and the time is right in which to do it. Obviously, you shouldn't dowse if you're angry, depressed, hungover, unwell, or have an emotional investment in the outcome. Many dowsers also ask: "Will the answers I receive be correct?"

You can also ask questions to help protect yourself. You can ask if you're sufficiently grounded and have enough energy to perform the dowsing.

You can use your pendulum to increase your energy if you get a negative response to this question. All you need to do is to spin your pendulum in clockwise circles and ask it to raise your energy to its highest level. You can increase your energy this way whenever you need it.

## How to Ask Questions

As your pendulum provides only four responses, you need to phrase your questions carefully. You can't, for instance, ask your pendulum, "Should I spend my vacation in Las Vegas or San Francisco?" You could ask the question twice, once for Las Vegas, and again for San Francisco. Alternatively, you could ask, "Would it be better for me to fly to Las Vegas rather than San Francisco?" If you wanted to, you could confirm the result by asking the question again with the possible destinations reversed.

Vague questions can't be answered by your pendulum, either. "Will I be successful in my career?" is an example. The word "successful" is too vague: Do you mean successful in terms of becoming CEO of a large company, or would you consider someone who is manager of a small corporation successful in a different way? Would you consider success solely in financial terms? If you're a teacher, success might be measured by the number of people you've helped or the respect and appreciation you receive from others. The question also fails to consider possible changes in career you might make as you go through life.

It's generally better to ask a series of simple questions rather than coming up with a complex question that will answer all your questions with one swing of your pendulum. If you want to speed up the process, you can use phrases such as "instead of," "in preference to," or "rather than." Here's an example: "Should I go to Maui for my summer vacation rather than Portland, Oregon?"

Every now and again, your pendulum will give you the "I don't want to answer" response. It could mean that you didn't ask the question clearly enough and need to reframe it. And sometimes there's a genuine reason (that you're probably aware of) as to why your pendulum doesn't want to answer your question. If you feel your question prompted the response, think of your intention again and ask two or three simpler questions that will lead you to the answer.

It's important to focus on your question while holding your pendulum. If you start thinking about other things while holding the pendulum, it may respond to an idle thought rather than your question. With practice, you'll find that it won't take long before you automatically enter into a state where your mind is still and you're able to focus solely on the question.

It's important to be well-hydrated when dowsing. In a study conducted in the 1960s, Dr. Harvalik found that people's dowsing ability improved if they drank a few tumblers of water" before starting (Wilson 1988, 116).

## What Questions to Ask First

The best way to start is to ask your pendulum questions that you already know the answers to. You might ask: "Is my name (whatever it happens to be)?" "Am I married?" "Do I have three children?" "Do I drive a (particular type of vehicle)?" "Have I ever traveled to Zanzibar?" Take as much time as necessary and your pendulum will answer "yes" or "no" to each of these questions.

The purpose of asking questions you already know answers to is to help you get used to the movements of your pendulum and to verify that it is giving you correct answers. Some people get wrong answers to questions of this sort when they're first starting to use their pendulum, but there's no need to be concerned if it happens to you. As you get familiar with your pendulum and start feeling comfortable with it, you'll find that your accuracy will improve until you get correct responses every time.

You can ask your questions silently or out loud. I ask questions aloud when I'm with a client, as I want them to know what I'm doing. However, I usually think of the question when I'm dowsing for my own purposes.

After your pendulum has correctly responded to all the questions for which you already know the answers, you can start asking it questions that you don't already know the answers to. Start by asking questions that you can check quickly and easily. You might ask: "Is my partner currently driving home from work?" Make a note of the time you asked the question and confirm the answer when your partner arrives home. Before going to visit someone's home for the first time, you might ask: "Does (friend's name) have a cat?"

The next step is to start asking questions that you may not be able to check instantly. There is one caveat to this, the fact that you can overrule your pendulum's responses with your mind. Here's a common example. Let's assume you're dowsing to determine the sex of an unborn baby. If you secretly hope it will be a girl, your pendulum will respond to your desire and confirm that the baby will be a girl, even if that is not correct. In a situation of this sort, it's better to ask someone who has no emotional involvement in the outcome to hold the pendulum and ask the question. It may seem that your pendulum is deliberately lying to you in cases like this. However, the response comes from your subconscious mind, which is constantly looking after you. When this happens, your subconscious mind is trying to protect you from information that you may not be prepared for or be willing to hear.

You can prove to yourself that you can move the pendulum with the power of your mind. Suspend your pendulum and stop its movements with your free hand. Once you've done that, remove your hand and ask the pendulum to move in a particular direction. After a few seconds, the pendulum will start to move in the direction you're thinking about. Start willing it to move in another direction, and it will respond to your thought and change to indicate the new direction.

Your pendulum is a serious device and shouldn't be used frivolously. If you treat it as a toy and ask flippant questions, you'll receive the responses you deserve. If, for instance, you ask your pendulum, "Am I incredibly beautiful?" you might receive an honest answer (yes or no). You could receive the answer you want to hear because you have the ability to override your pendulum's response. You're more likely to receive a mischievous answer ("I don't know" or "I don't want to answer"). Your pendulum might appear to shiver in your hand, which means it wants you to ask it serious questions.

Your pendulum may also give wrong answers if it senses you're being selfish or insincere. Your questions must be sincere, and you must always work for the highest good for everyone involved. Wrong answers can also occur when people around you are skeptical or insincere.

## Ethics

It's important to ask questions that are ethical. You can't ask the pendulum if someone's partner is having an affair, for instance. When you read for others, you're likely to be asked questions of this sort from time to time, and it's important to refuse to answer them. In addition, you must never ask questions that relate to other people unless they've given you permission to do so.

The next chapter contains several experiments to help you develop your skills.

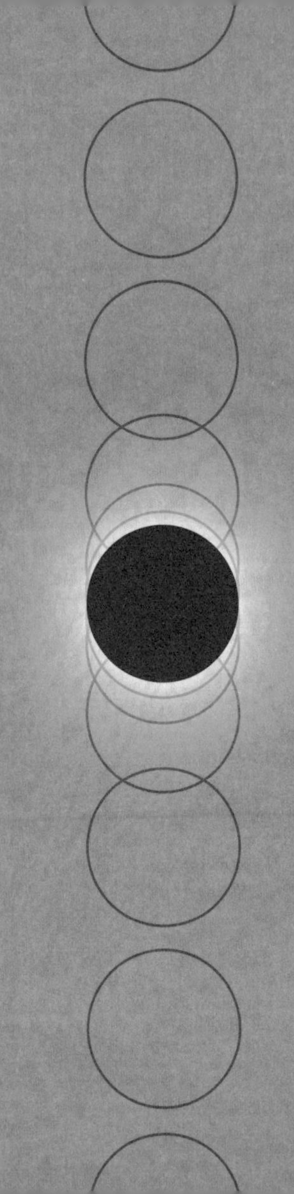

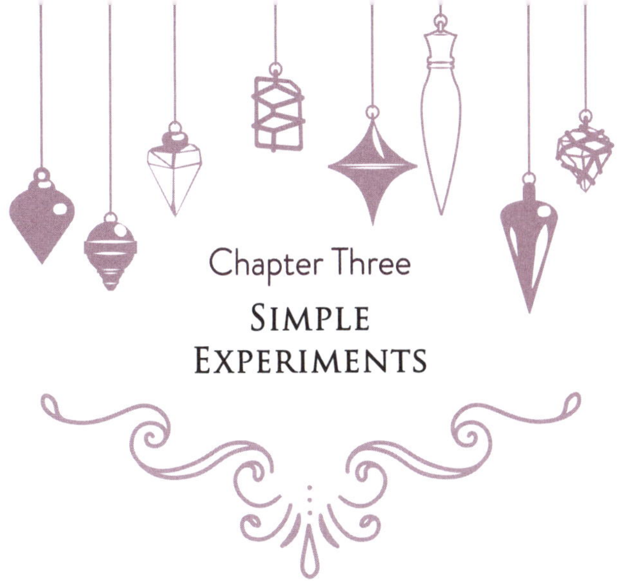

# Chapter Three
# Simple Experiments

Becoming an expert with the pendulum takes time; many experts say that it takes about a year to become proficient with it. However, this is only an approximation that depends on how frequently you practice with your pendulum. Fortunately and unlike many other skills, practicing with your pendulum is fun.

It's better to practice in short bursts. Ten or twenty minutes three times a week is better than one sixty-minute session every week, a discovery made in the early days of parapsychological research when scientists discovered that volunteers achieved better results at the start of their sessions than they did later on. They learned that the volunteers became bored after a while, which led to the decline of their success rate.

Don't worry if your pendulum gives the wrong answer or gives you an "I don't know" or "I don't want to answer" response. While you're learning, your pendulum will provide incorrect answers at times. It may sense that you don't feel confident about what you're doing, it may be picking up extraneous thoughts from your mind, or the movements might be too slight to interpret correctly. If you fail to get a correct response after three attempts, put your pendulum down for several minutes, drink a glass of water, and take several slow, deep breaths before trying again.

There are many tests and experiments that you can practice as you develop your pendulum skills, several of which are included here. The most famous is the Coué pendulum test.

It's best to practice each of these experiments two or three times and to then move on to another experiment. You don't need to be successful at each one before moving on to the next. The most important things are to adopt a lighthearted, positive approach and to continue only as long as your interest remains high.

## The Coué Pendulum Test

Emile Coué (1857–1926) was a French psychologist and hypnotist who gained international fame with an affirmation he created: "Every day, in every way, I am getting better and better." When he visited New York in 1923, thousands of people who had been helped by this affirmation were waiting on the docks to welcome him.

Emile Coué's pendulum test was devised to demonstrate concentration.

### • • • Exercise 2 • • •
### The Coué Pendulum Test

1. Start by drawing a circle approximately six inches in diameter. Draw two lines (one horizontal and one vertical) to divide the circle into quarters.
2. Suspend your pendulum over the center of the cross created by the two lines. Notice that your pendulum will start to move to follow one of the lines.

3. Visualize the strength of your pendulum's movement increasing and watch it happen.
4. Imagine the pendulum is slowing down until it stops.
5. Ask it to start moving to follow the other straight line. As before, visualize the movement of your pendulum increasing, and then ask it to slow down to a stop.
6. Close your eyes and ask the pendulum to follow the horizontal line. When you feel it is swinging strongly, open your eyes to confirm that it is following the horizontal line.
7. Close your eyes again and visualize your pendulum moving to follow the vertical line. When you sense that it is doing that, open your eyes to confirm that it is following the vertical line.
8. Close your eyes and visualize your pendulum moving in clockwise circles. Open your eyes to confirm that it is, and then close your eyes again and visualize it moving in counterclockwise circles.

9. Open your eyes and congratulate yourself on your excellent concentration.

## Across the Divide

All you need for this experiment is a sheet of 8½" × 11" paper, two coins of the same denomination, and your pendulum.

Place the two coins a few inches apart on the sheet of paper. Hold your pendulum between the two coins, and you'll find that after a few moments, it will start to swing from side to side between the two coins.

Put your pendulum down and draw a line with a pen or pencil across the paper between the two coins. Hold your pendulum over one of the coins. It should start to rotate around the coin. Once that movement is firmly established, slowly move the pendulum toward the other coin. As it gets close to the line you drew between the two coins, the pendulum's movements will change, beginning to move to and fro along the line instead of from side to side between the two coins. If you then suspend your pendulum over the other coin, you'll find it reacts in exactly the same way. Your pendulum will revolve around the coin and as you slowly move it toward the other coin it will follow the direction of the line. The line you drew acts as a physical barrier that prevents the pendulum from swinging freely between the two coins.

## The Circle Test

Draw a circle about six inches in diameter on a piece of paper. Next, draw two lines to make a cross that divides the circle into quarters. Hold your pendulum over the center of the cross and allow your pendulum to decide which of the two intersecting lines it would like to follow. Once it is moving in a particular direction, slowly move your pendulum along the line. When it reaches the curve marking the diameter of the circle, the pendulum will change direction. Mentally ask it to continue moving beyond the limits of the circle, and you'll find it will immediately stop moving. If you bring the pendulum back inside the circle it will start moving again. In this case, the diameter of the circle has created a barrier that prevents the pendulum from moving beyond it.

## Ruler Test

This test has some similarities to the Circle Test. You need a twelve-inch ruler for this experiment. Hold your pendulum over the center of the ruler and your pendulum will start to swing to and fro along the ruler's length. Once it's swinging freely, change the direction of the ruler and you'll find your pendulum will also change direction to continue swinging along the length of the ruler.

Next, slowly move the pendulum along the ruler. It will continue swinging back and forth until you reach the end of the ruler where it will start rotating. Once you start moving it back down the ruler it will start swinging along the ruler's length until you get to the other end where it will rotate again. However, you'll find that at this end it will rotate in the direction opposite to the rotation it did at the other end.

## Fruit Bowl

As well as a selection of several different fruits or vegetables, you'll need a friend to help you. Place the fruits in a line on a table. Tell your friend that you're going to turn your back, and while you're not looking, they should pick up one piece of fruit, hold it for a moment, and then put it exactly where it was before. Once they have done that, turn around, pick up your pendulum, and mentally ask it to let you know what item of fruit your friend selected. Take your time holding your pendulum over each piece of fruit in turn. It will give the same response to all of the fruits except for one, where the response will be noticeably different. This will be the fruit your friend selected.

You don't need to restrict yourself to fruits and vegetables. You can do this test with other objects too, such as coins and playing cards.

## Experiments with Playing Cards

Playing cards are a useful way to help you develop your connection with your pendulum. They're convenient, take up little room, and can be used whenever you have a few minutes to practice and become used to working with your pendulum.

Take a red card and a black card from a deck of playing cards. Mix them thoroughly face down so you have no idea which card is which. Decide on a color and focus on it while holding your pendulum over each card in turn and asking: "Is this card the red card?"

You should get a positive response over one card and a negative reaction over the other. Do not rush this test—give the pendulum enough time to give you a good positive or negative response over each card. Once you've done this, check to see if your pendulum has provided the correct answer.

# Problem Solving

It can be frustrating when you have difficulties connecting with your pendulum or fail to receive clear answers to your questions. There can be a number of reasons.

You might need to rephrase your question to make it clearer. You may have problems if you're physically unwell. In that case, put your pendulum aside until you feel well again. You should also set your pendulums aside if you're intoxicated, have consumed drugs, or are in emotionally intense states, such as anger, anxiety, or trauma. Your pendulum may protect you by not responding if your question relates to anything emotionally painful.

If you're dehydrated, a large glass of water will resolve the problem. Don't use your pendulum when skeptics are present as they can affect the movements of your pendulum.

Don't persist if your pendulum refuses to respond. Put it aside and try again later. If possible, take a walk to ground yourself and clear your mind.

You can extend this test by mixing one red card with three black cards. Hold your pendulum over each card in turn while asking, "Is this the red card?" Once you've succeeded with this, add more black cards and try again.

Another version of this uses the four aces in a deck of cards. Mix the cards face down and place them in a row in front of you. Decide which ace you want your pendulum to find and then hold it over each card in turn while asking, "Is this the Ace of Hearts (or whatever ace you are looking for)?" Once you've succeeded with this you might try to find all four aces, one at a time.

A more advanced test is to thoroughly mix a deck of cards and place it face down on a table in front of you. Hold your pendulum over the deck and ask, "Is the top card red?" Your pendulum will respond with a yes or no answer. If the pendulum gives a positive response place the top card, still face down, to one side of the deck of cards. Ask the same question for the next nine or ten cards, placing all the positive responses on one side of the deck and negative responses on the other. Stop when you feel like it and check to see how many cards your pendulum identified correctly.

## Correct or Incorrect

For this experiment you'll need several pieces of paper. Write down true statements about yourself on half of the sheets of paper. You might write: "I am (whatever it happens to be) years old." "I live at (your correct address)." "I work as a (whatever it happens to be)." "My partner's name is (their name)."

On the other pieces of paper, write down statements that are incorrect. Last year I traveled to (a place you've never visited)." "My first name is (incorrect name)." "I love eating (a food that you strongly dislike)." "I have (incorrect number) children."

Mix up the sheets of paper and lay them out face down in a row in front of you. Hold your pendulum over each piece of paper in turn while asking, "Is this statement the truth?"

Your pendulum will respond positively or negatively. Once you've dowsed all the pieces of paper, turn them over to check your pendulum's accuracy.

## Where to Go on Vacation

I read somewhere that most people spend more time planning their annual vacation than they do thinking about their life goals. Your pendulum can help you choose the ideal place to have a good vacation. The first step is to make a list of all the possibilities you have in mind and are within your budget.

Hold your pendulum over each name on your list in turn and ask it if you'd have an enjoyable vacation there. As these are all the places you'd like to visit, the chances are you'll receive a positive answer for all of them.

The next step is to determine which destination would give you the most enjoyable vacation. Start by holding your pendulum over the first item on your list and ask: "I'm going to be on vacation from (date) to (date). Would I have a better vacation at (first place on your list) than I would have at (second place on your list)?" If you get a negative response, hold your pendulum over the second item on your list and ask: "I'm going to be on vacation from (date) to (date). Would I have a better vacation at (second place on your list) than I would have at (first place on your list)?" If you receive a no response, it means you'll have just as much fun at both destinations. A positive response means you'll now know which of the two destinations would be better for you. Now you need to ask the same questions with the third destination on your list. By the time you've finished going through your list, you'll have found the destination that will be best for you.

## Predicting the Future

An interesting test for your pendulum is to ask it to predict the outcome of events that will happen in the near future. You might, for instance, ask your pendulum if it will rain tomorrow, or if your favorite team will win their game tonight. However, it's not a good idea to use your pendulum to predict future events if you're planning to bet on the outcome. Whenever I've tried to do this, my pendulum has given me "I don't know" or "I don't want to answer" responses.

Don't be disheartened if your accuracy rate isn't high to begin with. It's important to remain positive. If you keep a record of your pendulum's predictions, you'll find that your accuracy rate will steadily improve over time as you gain experience with it.

## Everyday Decisions

You can ask your pendulum questions about almost anything, such as what meal to have for dinner, what clothes to wear, and what route to take to work. At the end of the day, check to see how useful your pendulum was in helping you make decisions.

## Character Analysis

You can ask your pendulum questions about people you'll shortly be meeting to gain information about their character, honesty, integrity, and anything else you want to know. It's useful to ask questions about people's character and integrity, but it's not acceptable to ask personal questions about anyone without their consent, and using your pendulum to probe into other people's lives is highly unethical. If, for instance, you've applied for a job, you can learn information about the person who'll be interviewing you. Before you go on a blind date, you can learn about the person and their character ahead of time. If you need a tradesperson to repair something in your home, you can choose the right person by asking your pendulum about the person or people you have in mind.

The next chapter covers how to use your intuition as well as your pendulum to gain information about anything you wish situated far away from where you happen to be. This is called distant dowsing or, more commonly, map dowsing.

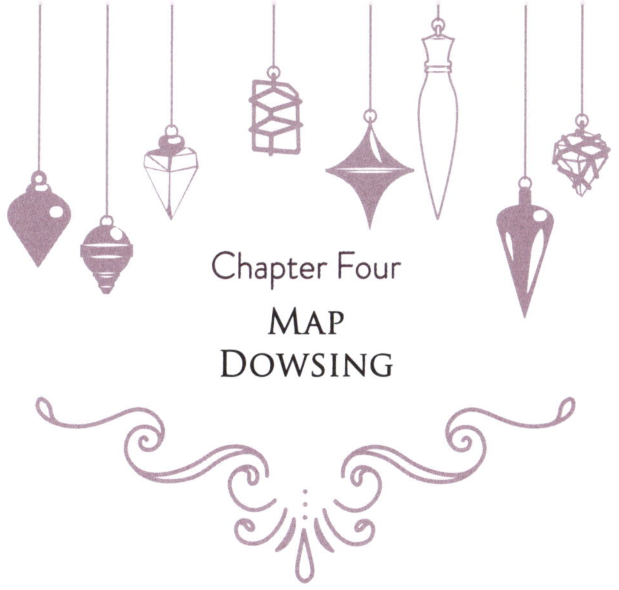

# Chapter Four
# Map Dowsing

Many people are able to dowse anywhere in the world from the comfort of their own home. This is called distant dowsing or map dowsing as they hold their pendulums over a chart or map instead of being at the site in person. Instead of a map, you can also use drawings, photographs, letters, signatures, or an object from the area you want to dowse.

The French priest mentioned in chapter 1, Abbé Mermet, located oil, minerals, and water in Africa and South

America. He did archaeological dowsing for the Vatican and found missing people using nothing but his pendulum.

In 1959, in front of a group of senior naval officers, Verne Cameron, a professional dowser in California, located the position of the entire US submarine fleet in the Pacific Ocean using his pendulum and a map. He also located every Russian submarine around the world. Several years later, when he tried to get a passport, it was declined: The Navy had told the CIA about Cameron's dowsing skills, and he was considered a security risk.

In 1986, *The Financial Times* in London reported that Uri Geller earned one million dollars for every map dowsing assignment he undertook (Jacobsen 2017, 332). Obviously, his success rate must have been high to earn that amount of money.

There are a number of ways to perform map dowsing. They all begin by orienting your map to true north. Let's assume you're trying to find someone's missing pet. The first method is to hold your pendulum over a map of the area where the pet is thought to be and see if your pendulum indicates the path the lost animal took.

The second method is to hold a pencil in your free hand and to use it as a pointer. Your other hand holds the pendulum to one side. Slowly move the pointer over the map. As you do this, your pendulum will provide you with positive and negative responses.

Another method is to slowly move the pendulum along the horizontal and vertical edges of a map while asking it to indicate where the missing pet (or whatever you are looking for) happens to be. Mark the places the pendulum indicates and, using a ruler, draw a horizontal and vertical line to pinpoint where the pet is.

While using any of these methods, ask as many questions as necessary: "Was the pet traveling on its own?" "Did he or she turn right at the crossroads?" The answers to your questions will provide additional information that will help you find the missing pet.

Some fortunate people are able to map dowse right away, but most people have to develop their skills through practice. A good way to start is to obtain a map of your local area. Hold your pendulum over your home and ask it to lead you to a friend's house, or maybe a particular store, school, park, or somewhere else you enjoy visiting. If you know a friend is somewhere within the area shown by the map, you can ask your pendulum to indicate where they are. Once it has, get in touch with your friend to see if your pendulum's response was accurate.

If you want to move to another area, you can map dowse to find the perfect place for you to live. Make sure to list all the requirements you need in the new location and then let your pendulum find it for you. A friend of mine moved from the United Kingdom to New Zealand several years ago and used his pendulum to find the city that would be best for him and his family. He then asked for the best suburb for his budget. Finally, he asked for the best possible streets in the suburb. All of this was done three months before he and his family moved half-way around the world. Within weeks of arriving, they bought a house perfect for their needs. This shows that you can map dowse anywhere in the world.

Some years ago, a dowsing society I belong to conducted an interesting experiment. We were all given a map of the area the meeting was held in, and one member was told to drive to any place he chose within the area on the map. He was to stand beside his car for five minutes and to then start walking in any direction he wished, preferably using a number of suburban streets rather than walking in a straight line. While he was doing this, the rest of the group used their pendulums to find out where he parked his car and then trace the route he walked on their maps. The only instructions we were given were to focus on the person we were to track and then see if we could find him with our pendulums. The first people to announce that they'd found a location did it by slowly moving their pendulums from the top right-hand side of the map down to the bottom while asking the pendulum to indicate when it had found the person. Once they had these coordinates, they repeated the process using the bottom edge of the map from one side to the other until the pendulum reacted. The place where the two imaginary lines crossed was where the society member was standing beside his car. Once he started moving, it was a simple matter to follow the route he took by holding the pendulum over the route as he moved.

The members who did not use the coordinates method either divided the map into smaller sections and asked about each in turn (the grid method) or used the triangulation method, which involves placing the pendulum over one of the bottom corners of the map and asking the pendulum to indicate the direction of the man and his car. Once the pendulum has indicated a specific direction, you can use a ruler to mark the direction. If this is repeated from the other bottom corner, the person will be where the two lines intersect.

## Question to Ask When Looking for a New Home

- Is now a good time for me to move?
- Is this (town or city) the right place for me to live in?
- Would I be happy living in (a particular neighborhood)?
- Is (neighborhood) quiet?
- Will I find supportive neighbors and new friends in (neighborhood)?
- Is (location) good for my lifestyle and work considerations?
- Is (specific address) the right place for me?
- Will I feel safe and secure living at (specific address)?
- Will my (partner, family, boarders, pets) be happy living at (specific address)?
- Is (specific address) within walking distance of (your specific requirements, such as library, school, park, and convenience stores)?
- Is it within my budget?
- Is there another place that I haven't considered that would be better for me?

This was a popular exercise; almost every member succeeded in finding the man and tracking the route he took. Although we did this as a group, you can perform this experiment with a friend. If your friend is genuinely interested in dowsing rather than merely being supportive, you could take turns in walking and tracking.

Whenever possible, use published maps when you're map dowsing. Hand-drawn maps, charts and diagrams work well, but if they're not drawn to scale, you may pinpoint a position that is feet, yards, or even miles from whatever it is you are dowsing for. Even better is using two or three maps when you can. A small-scale map will let you dowse a large area but makes it difficult to determine positions exactly. One solution is to take a photograph of a section of the small-scale map and enlarge it so that you can dowse more accurately once you get close to whatever it is you are dowsing for.

Sometimes when map dowsing with a pointer, you'll find it moving away from the edge of the map. This means that whatever you are dowsing for is on an adjacent map. If you don't have one, place a blank sheet of paper next to the map and draw the movements of the pointer onto it. The only times you're likely to find this necessary is when you're tracking the movements of a missing person or pet, or when following the course of an underground stream.

### • • • Exercise 3 • • •
### *How to Dowse Photographs*

Your pendulum will help you receive answers to questions about someone using a photograph of him or her. There must be only one person in the photograph and no pets or other animals to ensure that any questions you ask relate only to the subject of the photograph.

Write down the questions you want to ask the person in the photograph. You might want to ask: "Are you currently alive?" I ask this even if the photograph appears to be extremely old. You can continue with: "Are you currently married?" If the person is deceased, you might ask: "Were you married?" You can continue by asking about the person's family, children, location, occupation, and anything else you want to know.

1. Start by asking your pendulum the "Can I?", "May I?", and "Should I?" questions.
2. Hold your pendulum in your usual hand and hold the palm of your other hand an inch or two above the photograph. Ask the

pendulum to tell you when your free hand is at the optimum height over the photograph to receive information. Slowly raise your free hand until your pendulum tells you to stop.

3. Ask the pendulum your first question. If you know the name of the person in the photograph, you can include it in the question. You might ask: "Is (name of person) currently alive?"
4. Continue asking questions until you've gained all the information you want.
5. Finish by swinging your pendulum in clockwise circles while thanking the person in the photograph for their help.

Many people who believe in dowsing still find it hard to accept that it's possible to dowse by holding a pendulum over a map. In truth, map dowsing is a form of clairvoyance. The pendulum acts as an extension to our central nervous system, which is able to contact the universal mind and find the answer. This is why we can go to bed with a problem on our mind and wake up in the morning with the answer. While we were asleep, our subconscious mind worked on the problem and received an answer from the universal mind. Fortunately, it doesn't matter if you believe in map dowsing, or not. All you need do is to temporarily suspend any disbelief and trust the movements of your pendulum.

Everyone's experienced the frustration of losing something and being unable to find it. Fortunately, your pendulum is a practical tool that will help you find anything that is missing or lost, the subject of the next chapter.

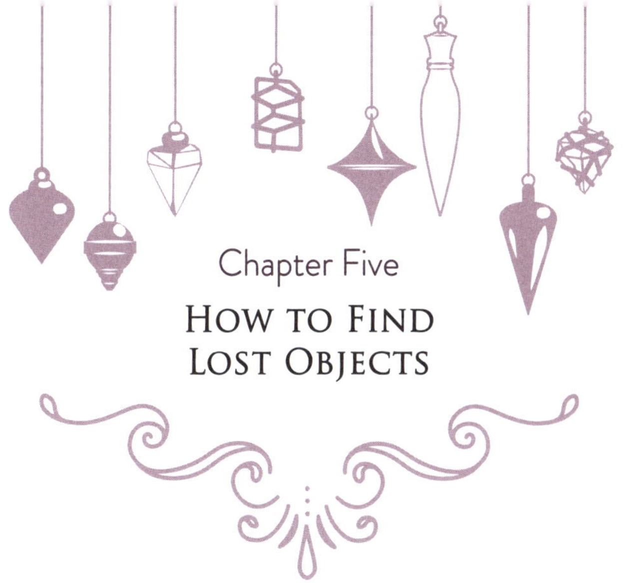

Chapter Five

# How to Find Lost Objects

We've all lost things at times and experienced a sense of panic when we couldn't find whatever it happened to be, especially if it was something important like house or car keys. Often, you're likely to be in a hurry anyway, making a bad situation worse.

The first and most important thing to do is to calm down and relax. This isn't easy when you're stressed, but it's vital to be relaxed when using your pendulum. Start the process by sitting down and drinking a glass of water.

Follow this by taking several slow, deep breaths. If you have a smartwatch, you might be able to check that your heart rate has returned to normal.

When you feel reasonably relaxed, pick up your pendulum and ask it a question that you think you already know the answer to. If, for instance, you've mislaid your car keys and are reasonably sure they're inside your house, you could ask, "Are my car keys inside the house?" If they are, your pendulum will give a positive response. It's good news if they are, as you can then narrow the search and dowse your home room by room. It's also helpful to get a negative response, as you'll know your keys are outside and you can ask further questions, such as, "Are they in the car?"

Continue asking questions until you've found the missing object. Sometimes just asking the question will be enough. You might ask, "Are the car keys in the dining room?" and will instantly remember placing them on furniture in that room.

There's another method you can use once you've reduced the search to a single room. Stand in the doorway and ask your pendulum to locate the missing item. It will start swinging to indicate the direction the object is in. Move to another part of the room and ask the same question. Your pendulum will swing to indicate where the object is from where you're standing. The missing object will be found where the two invisible lines intersect.

You don't need to wait until you've lost something to practice finding it. Ask a family member to hide a small object somewhere in your home and then use your pendulum to find it. Start by asking if the object is in, say, the family room. If your pendulum says "no," ask if it's in various rooms until you get a positive response. Go to that room and continue asking questions, such as "Is it in the closet?," "Is the object visible from where I'm standing?," and "Is it under a piece of furniture?" until you locate the hidden item.

Alternatively, you might mentally split the room into four quarters and ask about each one in turn. Once you know what quarter of the room the object is in, you can mentally divide that quarter into four smaller quarters and find the item that way.

An alternative method is to stand in two different places in the room and ask your pendulum to swing to indicate where the object is. Ask the question again while standing somewhere else in the room. The object will be found where the two invisible lines intersect. This is called the triangulation method as the two invisible lines make up two sides of a triangle.

This is a useful experiment, as the chances are high that you and other members of your family will lose something one day. When it happens, your pendulum will help you find it.

A more advanced method to find something that you know is somewhere inside your house is to slowly walk from room to room with your pendulum suspended from your hand. While doing this, focus on your need for whatever the lost object is. The pendulum will start swinging as you get close to the missing item, and the swinging motion will become more vigorous the closer you get to it. This method is more difficult than the others as you need to be well attuned to your pendulum to recognize the movements when they start to occur.

You can also find a lost object by map dowsing for it. If you know the object is inside your house you can draw an approximate floor plan and hold your pendulum over each room in turn. After it has found the room that the object is in you can ask further questions until you discover the exact location.

## Can't Find Your Pendulum?

There's no need to panic if you lose your pendulum. Start by looking in the places where you usually keep your pendulum, and check that it hasn't slipped behind or under something nearby.

If that doesn't solve the problem, make an impromptu pendulum using a length of string and a small weight, such as a ring or washer. It will work like your regular pendulum, and you can ask it a series of questions that will lead you to your missing pendulum. You might start by asking: "Is my pendulum inside the house/apartment?" If you get a positive response, you can ask more questions until you find what room it is in. That might be all you need, but you can ask further questions, if necessary, to help you locate the exact position.

If your impromptu pendulum tells you that it's not in the house, ask it questions about places you've visited recently. If that doesn't produce a result, hold it over a map of the area and map dowsing will indicate where your pendulum is (see previous chapter).

Some years ago, a school principal told me how he drew a chart of his school to find a folder of important papers he had misplaced. There were dozens of rooms in the school, but once he'd drawn a rough chart, it took him only a few minutes to find the papers. A day or two earlier, he'd put the papers down on a workbench in the school's storage room while having a brief conversation with the school caretaker.

You can also practice finding things outdoors. A good way to start is to mark out a section of grass approximately ten feet square. Ask a friend to place a coin or other small object somewhere within this area. Tell them to place it somewhere where the height of the grass will make it hard to see. Stand outside one corner of the square you marked out and ask your pendulum to indicate the direction the coin is. Repeat this from an adjacent corner to create two invisible lines (the triangulation method). Once you've done this, go to the position where the two lines cross and pick up the coin. As far as your dowsing skills are concerned, this is an important exercise. You may have beginner's luck and find the coin right away, but you're more likely to make several attempts before you succeed. Continue practicing and you'll find your success rate will steadily increase.

Once you start having more successes than failures, you can increase the size of your search area, and continue the experiment on different types of terrain. If you do this in a sandy area, your friend can hide the coin just under the surface.

The next chapter covers the one thing that most people know about dowsing: How to find underground water using a pendulum.

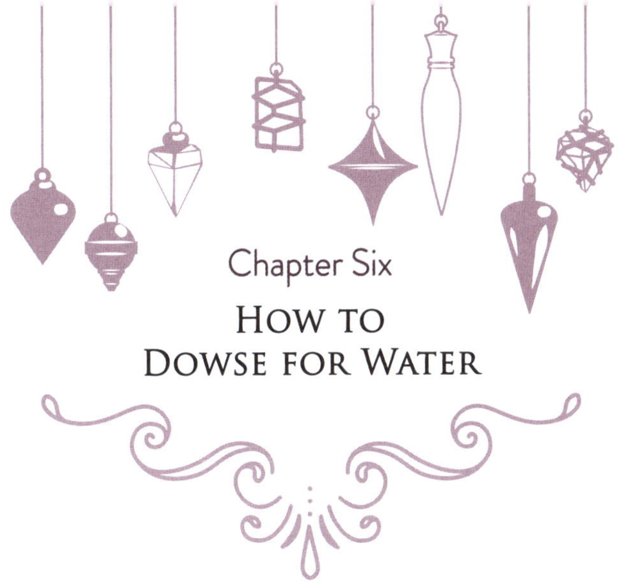

# Chapter Six
# How to Dowse for Water

When most people think of dowsing, the first thing that comes to mind is a person holding a forked stick or a pendulum while looking for underground water, a process called water divining or water witching. It's been practiced for thousands of years and is even mentioned in the Bible as Moses found water using a rod (Exodus 17:1–7). Other possible references to dowsing in the Bible can be found at Hosea 4:12, Psalm 125:3, Numbers 17:1–11, and Numbers 20:1–12.

It's not surprising that dowsers are regularly asked to find underground water—it's essential for all life as we know it. Just as important is finding pure water that can be drank safely. Fortunately, this is something that you can do with your pendulum.

Some people are naturally good at locating water with a pendulum, but anyone can do it with practice. Here's an example of someone who located water within fifteen minutes of dowsing for the first time. The leaders of Swampscott, Massachusetts, searched for almost twenty years to find a good supply of drinking water to replace the source they had lost. Nothing seemed to work, and the residents got tired of having water rationed every summer. In desperation, someone suggested dowsing. The Superintendent of Public Works, Paul A. Polisson, was skeptical, but the situation was desperate so he was willing to try anything. One morning, some local residents started dowsing in a group. Fifteen minutes after they started, a local laborer called Dutch Emery found a replacement supply of water with a dowsing response that was so strong it scraped skin off his thumb. Mr. Emery was a complete amateur who had never tried dowsing until that day.

## Some Rules for Dowsing

Take several slow deep breaths to help you relax and clear your mind before dowsing.

Set your intention.

Don't trespass on other people's property. Always ask for permission first.

Watch where you're going when walking with your pendulum.

Walk slowly and respond to your pendulum's movements. It can be a sign that you're getting closer to underground water when the movements of your pendulum become stronger.

If your pendulum indicates a particular direction, follow its movements as it could be leading you toward your target.

Once you've located water, ask specific questions about the depth of the water and its quality.

Trust in the process and follow your intuition.

Remain humble, patient, and grateful, no matter how experienced you become as a dowser.

### • • • Exercise 4 • • •
### *How to Find Water*

A useful way to develop your skills at dowsing for water is to find and then track a buried water line. This is easy to do if you live on a residential street in a suburban area.

The first step is to set your intention. In this case, your intention is to find an underground source of water. Depending on what you're going to be using the water for, you might set an intention to find a supply of underground water that is suitable for human consumption.

If you're dowsing a small area, you can start in one corner and walk from side to side in a zigzag pattern while thinking about your need to locate water. Each time your pendulum gives a positive response, place a peg in the ground at that spot. By the time you have finished walking over the area, you'll have a number of pegs in the ground that will mark out the course of a water pipe or underground stream.

This process works well if you're dowsing a small area but is impractical, not to mention time-consuming, if you're dowsing larger areas that could be a hundred acres or more.

When dowsing a large area, stand on one side of the location you're preparing to dowse instead of walking over the area. Hold your pendulum in your usual hand and extend your other hand out in front of you with your fingers touching and palm facing downward.

Take a few slow, deep breaths as you think about your intention, making sure to include what quality of water you're searching for. Slowly move your left hand across your target area. When your hand is pointing in the right direction your pendulum will start to gyrate. Once you know the direction of the water source, ask your pendulum, "How far away is the water vein?" Start counting in units that are appropriate to the size of the area you're dowsing. I usually use ten feet. Consequently, I'll count, "Ten feet? (pause) Twenty feet (pause) Thirty feet? (pause)" until the pendulum responds.

Once you've found the direction and approximate distance, walk in that direction. Slow down as you get near to the distance and mark the spot your pendulum indicates with a peg.

You can find the course of the water vein by moving thirty feet away from the peg and walking around it in a circle. The pendulum will react twice—mark both of these positions with pegs. If you need greater accuracy, you can repeat this step with larger circles.

Once you've found a vein of suitable water, you can use your pendulum to determine how far underground the water vein is. "Is the water ten feet down?" you might ask. "Is it twenty feet down?" Continue asking questions until your pendulum responds. Once this happens, you can stop there or be more specific if you wish. If your pendulum reacted at one hundred and twenty feet, you could ask: "Is the water vein at one hundred and fifteen feet? One hundred and sixteen? One hundred and seventeen?" Your pendulum will react somewhere between one hundred and fifteen feet and one hundred and twenty feet, giving you the correct depth to within one foot.

Another method is to stand over the position that your pendulum indicated and to walk on the spot. Each step you make indicates one foot of depth. Experiment with both and see which method you prefer.

The next step is to determine how much water is passing through the vein. This is important, as it will be a waste of time to drill a well if the yield is small. You do this by standing over the vein and asking your pendulum: "How many gallons of water per minute will this vein provide? Ten gallons? Twenty gallons" Thirty gallons?" Your pendulum will respond at the nearest ten gallons.

The final stage of the process is to determine the quality of the water you've found. Ask your pendulum if the water is the quality you requested for before starting. It should give a positive response to this. After this, ask if it exceeds this quality. It's always a happy moment to receive a positive answer to this question.

You now know the quality, yield, and depth of the water. Look around to see if it's a suitable place to drill a well. If it isn't, you can follow the vein until you find a place that is more convenient to place the well. Once you've found it, ask the questions again to confirm that the new site is as good or even better than where you first located water.

It takes time and practice to become good at dowsing for water. Many dowsers are able to find water but are unable to accurately determine the depth, yield, or quality of the potential well. Even experts make mistakes at times. These mistakes are usually caused by failing to ask the correct questions. A famous example of this involved Colonel K. W. Merrylees, an extremely successful dowser and the second president of the British Society of Dowsers.

On one occasion he successfully located water and also gauged the depth and quantity. However, he neglected to ask about the quality. The well produced 22,000 gallons of water per hour but was too salty for the agricultural use it had been drilled for (Bell 1965, 98–99).

Nothing could be more important than our health, and in the next chapter we'll look at a number of ways in which your pendulum can help you, your friends, and even your pets, maintain good health.

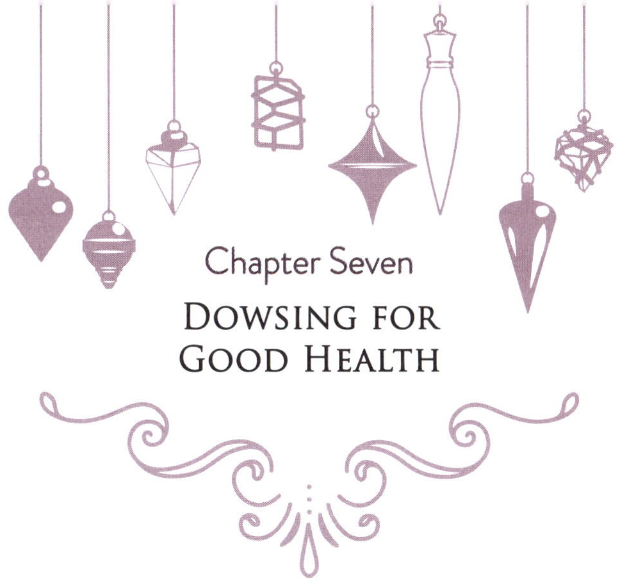

# Chapter Seven

# Dowsing for Good Health

You, like every other person on this planet, need food, water, air, and shelter to survive. Once those basic needs are met, you also need good mental and physical health to make the most of this lifetime and to live life to the fullest. Many people take their health for granted until a major accident or illness occurs, when health suddenly becomes their main priority. It's important that you make all health-related decisions only after they've been evaluated by your doctor. However, you can use your pendulum to point out any areas you should be concerned about and then schedule an appointment with your doctor to check everything out.

## How to Test Foods

It can be an interesting experiment to hold your pendulum over a variety of foods and drinks and ask it if the particular item would be beneficial for you to consume now. It's important to include the final word "now." This is because something that might normally be good for you ceases to be beneficial if you have already eaten too much food.

While doing this exercise, try holding your pendulum over a cigarette, a noxious weed, a recreational drug, a spoonful of sugar, and anything you're allergic to or are addicted to. Record the results.

Now place a selection of fresh fruits and vegetables in a row in front of you and test each one with your pendulum. Again, record the results.

Finally, hold your pendulum over a cup of coffee, a bar of chocolate, a glass of water, a glass of soda, and your favorite beverage.

After recording the results of the final items, you might find that your pendulum has given a positive response to all the items you thought would be good for you and a negative response to the others. However, you might have one or even a number of surprises and find that something you thought would be good for you to consume now in fact isn't, and something you thought would be bad is not, at least at this very moment. The first time I did this test I was surprised to discover that my pendulum rejected coffee, which I was drinking far too much of at the time. Given what the pendulum indicated, I gradually reduced the amount of coffee I consumed. I still drink it occasionally but nowadays prefer green tea.

You can repeat this experiment whenever you wish using as many foods and drinks as you like. It can be interesting to compare home-baked cookies to similar cookies bought from a supermarket, for instance. Compare raw vegetables with cooked vegetables. Organic vegetables with cheaper supermarket vegetables. It can be interesting to learn what your pendulum tells you about different meats.

The purpose of this experiment is to show you just how useful your pendulum can be in deciding what foods and drinks are good for you and which ones aren't. As everyone is different, you'll discover that the foods that are best for you may not be exactly the same as the foods your pendulum selects for someone else in your household.

If you take milk in your tea and coffee, you can ask your pendulum if you need the milk. If it says that you do, hold your pendulum in one hand while slowly pouring milk into your cup with your other hand. Your pendulum will tell you when to stop. Before drinking tea or coffee, ask your pendulum if it will be good for you. If you take sugar, perform this same test to find out what your pendulum has to say about it.

You can also test foods for possibly harmful food colorants, preservatives, and chemicals. Many fruits and vegetables are sprayed with pesticides, and your pendulum will detect the presence of the most harmful ones so you can avoid buying them or wash them thoroughly before testing them again and eating them if they're safe to eat. A friend of mine tests foods that have passed their use-by date to see if they can still be consumed.

There are many brands and varieties of milk available on supermarket shelves, and your pendulum can determine which is the best one for you. You can use your pendulum to determine which one has the highest nutritional value and to discover which has the fewest additives.

As well as testing food and drink that you think might be bad for you, you can also hold your pendulum over any food or drink you're planning to consume and ask, "Is this food for my highest and greatest benefit?"

A friend of mine is allergic to MSG (monosodium glutamate), a popular flavor enhancer, and has been hospitalized several times as a result of consuming it. Consequently, she phones the restaurant that interests her and asks if they use MSG. If they do, she thanks them and hangs up. Calling the restaurant is her first step. Because she has been ill after eating at restaurants that assured her they didn't use MSG, she has two further steps she takes. Before visiting any restaurant, she asks her pendulum if that particular establishment uses MSG or any other flavor enhancer when preparing their meals. She eats only at restaurants that her pendulum gives a negative response to this question, and when she's there she asks her pendulum to confirm the absence of MSG in any items on the menu that interest her.

As well as food, you can test the household products you usually buy to make sure they don't contain harmful chemicals.

## Are You Well-Balanced?

This exercise helps you determine how well-balanced the physical, mental, emotional, and spiritual aspects of your being are.

Start by drawing a circle divided into quarters. Write one aspect of your being in each quadrant. When you've done that, suspend your pendulum over the center of the circle and ask if all four areas of your being are in balance. If the answer is yes, you've successfully finished this exercise. Chances are, however, that won't be the case; it's extremely rare to find anyone who is perfectly balanced in all four areas. If your pendulum detected any imbalances, place it over each quadrant in turn and ask if it is balanced. Someone who overreacts every time he or she feels emotional is unlikely to be well-balanced in that area of life, and someone who lives on junk foods and neglects his or her physical body will not be well-balanced physically.

There may also be times when the pendulum's negative response comes as a surprise. You may think you're mentally well-balanced, for instance, but if you're constantly cynical or pessimistic, your pendulum may let you know that it's time to develop a more positive outlook.

Naturally you should act on what your pendulum says. It will also give you suggestions on how you can create balance in the quadrant or quadrants that are out of balance. You could ask it about different types of exercise, for instance, if your physical quadrant is out of balance. You may need to ask it many questions to determine what the problem is if your emotional quadrant is out of balance, as this could be caused by many different things—stress, overwork, or worries about a relationship.

## Physical Fitness

Your pendulum can help you keep in shape. You can ask it questions about different diets and physical fitness programs to see which ones will be beneficial for you. I helped my son find a gym from a list of possibilities. It suited him perfectly, and he's still a member after more than twenty years. A friend of mine wasn't happy when his pendulum told him he wasn't gaining many health benefits from his weekly game of golf. Apparently, the way he played the game was a leisure activity rather than exercise. After more questions, his pendulum told him that jump rope was the best exercise for him. His physical fitness increased rapidly once he started the new exercise regimen.

Once you've found an exercise that you enjoy, your pendulum will give you advice on how long to exercise and how strenuous the exercise should be.

It's obvious that a diet that consists of nothing but red meat or burgers and fries will ultimately prove harmful, yet I've met many people who do eat like that. Your pendulum will be quick to advise you on which foods are good for you and which are bad.

## Emotional Health

Emotions are strong psychological feelings that play an important role in everyone's life. Good emotions, such as feelings of happiness, excitement, and love, increase the richness of life, while negative emotions do the opposite. Prolonged feelings of envy, fear, jealousy, and hate are harmful to your physical and mental well-being. Unless they are dealt with, they have the potential to destroy long term relationships and can even kill you. This is why forgiving someone for something they did to you benefits you. As the other person may not even know or care how much they hurt you, forgiveness is a gift that you give to yourself.

Everyone has problems with their emotions at times, and it's important to learn how to handle them. Fortunately, your pendulum can help you find appropriate responses whenever anything occurs that affects your emotional health.

## Spiritual Health

Many people today describe themselves as spiritual seekers looking for something beyond themselves to believe in. They've realized that they are spiritual beings who want a closer connection with the Divine.

A fascinating experiment is to sit down quietly with your pendulum and say: "I am divine love. I am universal love. I am a spiritual being." Your pendulum should give a positive response to this. If it fails to react or reacts negatively, use the words as an affirmation for a day or two and then say them again while holding your pendulum. Continue doing this until your pendulum gives a positive response.

You can also ask your pendulum questions about different beliefs and religions. If you're moving to a new town or city, your pendulum will give you advice on what church, synagogue, or other place of worship would be best for you.

## Detecting Ill Health

Your pendulum can detect illnesses well before you realize you're unwell. It can also be used to determine the primary causes of health problems, as symptoms do not always indicate where the illness began. The following simple test shows you how your pendulum can scan your body to determine any areas of distress.

Sit down and suspend your pendulum over one of your knees. The pendulum will start moving, probably in clockwise circles. Put the pendulum down and give your knee a quick smack with the side of your hand. Suspend your pendulum over the same knee again and you'll find that either your pendulum won't move at all or will revolve in the opposite direction. It will take several minutes before your pendulum returns to its normal response.

It's not a simple matter to heal yourself with a pendulum because you are intimately involved with the process. Everyone fears the worst when health concerns arise, and these thoughts and feelings can prevent us from getting an accurate diagnosis. In practice, I always consult my doctor whenever I feel unwell. If I want to know more, I'll ask a friend to use their pendulum to answer any questions I may have about my health. As my friends don't have much emotional involvement in how I heal (beyond me feeling better, of course), their questions are likely to receive more accurate answers than mine would. Your pendulum won't ever provide a medical diagnosis but can point out any areas you should be concerned about. You can then schedule an appointment with your doctor to check things out.

## Controlling Stress

Many years ago, someone told me that the only people who don't experience stress are in graveyards. There are two forms of stress: eustress and distress. Eustress is positive and creates optimism, motivation, enthusiasm, and excitement. Distress is the opposite, creating feelings of anxiety, overwhelm, hopelessness, and loss of quality of life. When prolonged, it can cause depression and a variety of other health problems. Fortunately, your pendulum can help you lower your stress levels whenever necessary.

### • • • Exercise 5 • • •
### *Lower Your Stress Levels*

Sit down quietly somewhere where you won't be disturbed. Hold your pendulum in your dowsing hand and protect yourself, by asking the "Can I?", "Should I?", and "May I?" questions.

1. Tell your pendulum that you're feeling stressed and want to know where your stress levels are at the moment on a scale of one to ten.
2. Ask your pendulum: "Are my current stress levels higher than five?" If your pendulum gives a positive response, ask the same question again with the numbers six to ten until you receive a negative response.
3. Decide what level on the scale from one to ten you would like your stress levels to reduce to—one or two are both good options.
4. Spin your pendulum in clockwise circles as you close your eyes and take three slow, deep breaths. Visualize the positive movements of your pendulum steadily lowering your stress levels.
5. After a minute or two, open your eyes. Your pendulum may or may not still be rotating. Become aware of your body and how you

feel. You'll notice that your stress levels have reduced.

6. A lessening of your feelings of stress might be all that you need at this time. If so, you can finish the exercise at this point. If you wish, you can continue by asking your pendulum to tell you what level your stress levels are. If they're still higher than you desire, repeat the exercise again.

## Your Aura

Every living organism is surrounded by an electromagnetic energy field called the aura. In humans, the aura extends eight to ten feet in every direction. As the aura is present in every cell of the body, it is more correct to describe the aura as an extension of the body rather than an energy field that surrounds it.

The aura reveals a great deal about people's character, mentality, emotional state, health, vitality, and path through life. The aura retracts and expands in size depending on the health and well-being of the person. Someone who is physically fit, enthusiastic, and full of the joys of life has a much larger aura than someone who is frail and lacking in energy. When you spend time with a friend who is enthusiastic and cheerful, your aura expands as it reacts positively to your friend's radiant energy. Conversely, your aura is drained by people you dislike or have a negative attitude toward, which is why you feel tired and exhausted after being in their presence.

Every aura has a basic color that reveals the person's mental, emotional, and spiritual nature. In addition, rays of different colors emanate outward from the body containing all the colors of the rainbow. It's possible to determine someone's state of health and vitality by looking at the aura. Those who are physically well and full of life's joys have large, brightly colored auras. People who are unwell have smaller auras with colors that appear dull and unappealing.

With practice, anyone can learn to see auras, and you can also determine the colors and quality of people's auras by asking your pendulum about them. When you first experiment with this, you're likely to be surprised at how large people's auras are.

### • • • Exercise 6 • • •
### *How to Dowse for an Aura*

1. Ask a friend to stand with their arms and legs slightly apart. Stand about thirty feet behind your friend with your pendulum in

one hand and the palm of your other hand facing forward.

2. Tell yourself that you're dowsing for your friend's aura and would like your pendulum to respond when you reach the edge of the aura.
3. Slowly move toward your friend. You'll sense the edge of the aura through both the pendulum and the palm of your hand. You're likely to sense a slight resistance in the palm of your hand at the same time as your pendulum starts reacting.
4. After sensing the edge of the aura continue moving forward. You may feel a slight resistance from time to time as you pass through different layers of the aura. This resistance is likely to feel stronger when you get approximately two or three feet away from your friend. This inner layer of the person's aura is usually easier to sense than the outer edge.
5. Make a mental note of where you noticed the aura's outer edge, and then do this

exercise again from the person's front and sides. You'll find the aura extends just as far in each direction.

6. Walk around your friend and you'll find that the aura is a perfect circle that completely surrounds them.
7. Swap places and have your friend repeat the exercise. If possible, dowse for other people's auras as well. You can also dowse for the auras that surround your family pets.

As mentioned earlier, happy people who are full of energy and enthusiasm have auras that are large and vibrant. When the aura is small and in some cases seems to almost hug the body, the person may be unwell and may also lack confidence and energy and feel listless. Here is an exercise that demonstrates how you can use your pendulum to enlarge your aura and gain energy and enthusiasm.

## Suggestions on What You Can Dowse for Health

You can determine which foods, drinks, and supplements are good for you, and which to avoid.

You can test foods and drinks for artificial additives.

You can measure your stress levels and lower them, if necessary.

You can determine how well-balanced you are physically, mentally, emotionally, and spiritually.

You can determine how much exercise you need and choose an exercise program that works well for you and helps you achieve your goals.

You can dowse auras to determine someone's vitality and physical well-being.

You can balance chakras to correct any imbalances.

You can help people make good decisions about possible lifestyle changes to help their health and well-being.

You can determine the health and well-being of your pets.

### • • • Exercise 7 • • •

### *How to Influence Your Auric Field*

1. Start by sitting down comfortably. Take a few slow, deep breaths and then pick up your pendulum. Tell your pendulum that you want it to rate the size of your aura on a scale from one to ten. One means your aura is hugging your body and ten means it's as large as it ever gets. Ask your pendulum if it's happy to do this.
2. If it gives you a positive response, ask it if the size of your aura at the moment is larger than five. The answer to this will determine your next question. If you get a positive response, ask if it's higher than six, and continue asking about each number in turn until you get a negative response. Let's assume you get a negative response on number seven. As you know from your previous question that the number is higher than six but not higher than seven, you know that the size of your aura is currently seven. Confirm this by asking if it is number seven.

If you get a negative response to your first question (asking if it's higher than five), ask if it's lower than five, and continue going downward until you get a negative response. Ask the final question to confirm that you have the correct answer.

3. Put your pendulum down, close your eyes, and perform a relaxation exercise. You can do this in a number of ways. You can do a progressive relaxation by focusing on relaxing your toes and continuing by gradually moving up your body relaxing the muscles as go (toes, feet, calves, thighs, abdomen, chest, arms, neck, and head. You might prefer to take several slow and deep breaths while telling yourself that your aura is expanding with each exhalation. You might use a yogic breathing technique by inhaling through one nostril and exhaling through the other. A good way to do this is to close your right nostril with your right thumb. Inhale through your left nostril. Release your right thumb and use your right forefinger to close your left nostril. Exhale

through your right nostril. Keep the left nostril closed and inhale through your right nostril. Exhale through the same nostril, and then change your finger position to inhale and then exhale through the same nostril. While exhaling visualize your auric field growing in size. Ten breaths total should be enough to influence the size of your aura.

4. Open your eyes and pick up your pendulum again. Ask it if your aura is a higher number than it was when you first measured it. After relaxing and visualizing your aura expanding in size, it should be noticeably larger.
5. Ask your pendulum questions to determine how large it has become.

## The Chakras

Inside the aura and alongside the spinal column are seven revolving, wheel-like circles of energy that act as batteries that stimulate and energize the physical and subtle bodies they look after. They are called chakras, which is Sanskrit for "wheel."

Each chakra is related to a physical system and the organs associated with it. There is a direct relationship between the state of the chakra and the health of the organs it is responsible for. Chakras can be open, closed, blocked, and in or out of balance. Any changes made to the chakras to restore them to balance has an immediate effect upon the physical body.

It's unusual to find anyone with every chakra open and in balance. This fortunate person would feel joyful, happy, and fulfilled. Most people experience fluctuations in the state of their chakras due to fear, stress, and frustration.

## Root Chakra

**Color:** Red
**Element:** Earth
**Function:** Survival
**Glands:** Adrenals
**Sense:** Smell
**Desires:** Physical contact
**Keyword:** Physical

The root chakra is situated at the base of the spine in the area of the coccyx. It's often called the "base" chakra. It keeps us grounded to the earth, and is concerned with self-preservation, security, and comfort. It gives us vitality, energy, and a sense of really being alive. It symbolizes survival and the life force, and at an emotional level provides courage, strength, and persistence. It also looks after our sense of smell and the solid parts of our bodies, such as the teeth, bones, and nails.

An understimulated root chakra makes a person feel nervous and insecure, causing feelings of fear and problems with digestion. When the chakra is overstimulated, the person will be domineering, self-centered, and addicted to power, money, and sex.

### Sacral Chakra

**Color:** Orange
**Element:** Water
**Function:** Sexuality, creativity, pleasure
**Glands:** Ovaries, testes
**Sense:** Taste
**Desires:** Respect and acceptance
**Keyword:** Social

The sacral chakra is situated in the lower abdomen, approximately two inches below the navel. As it relates to the element of water, the sacral chakra is concerned with the body's fluidic functions. It represents creativity, emotional balance, and sexuality. It stimulates hope and optimism at an emotional level. It also relates to the sense of taste. A well-balanced sacral chakra in a person allows them to relate well with others, giving them the necessary fluidity to interact easily with everyone. If this chakra is blocked or understimulated, the person is likely to experience arthritis, urinary or sexual problems, as well as a loss of personal power. These problems are often caused by a buildup of negative emotions such as anger, frustration, and resentment. When the sacral chakra is overstimulated, the person will be aggressive, manipulative, and grossly self-indulgent.

### Solar Plexus Chakra

**Color:** Yellow
**Element:** Fire
**Function:** Will, personal power
**Glands:** Pancreas
**Sense:** Sight
**Desires:** To understand
**Keyword:** Intellect

The solar plexus chakra is situated between the navel and the sternum. It represents personal power, warmth, confidence, security, and happiness. It also provides good digestion and a feeling of physical well-being. It enhances creativity, optimism, trust, and self-respect at an emotional level. When the solar plexus chakra is overactive, the person will be an overly demanding, manipulative, perfectionist workaholic. When the solar plexus chakra is under stimulated, the person will lack confidence and ambition, be overly sensitive, and feel that he or she has virtually no control over circumstances or events.

### Heart Chakra

**Color:** Green
**Element:** Air
**Function:** Love
**Glands:** Thymus
**Sense:** Touch
**Desires:** To love and be loved
**Keyword:** Emotions

The heart chakra is situated in the center of the chest in line with the heart. It relates to personal and unconditional love, harmony, empathy, sympathetic understanding, compassion, healing, and the sense of touch. This is because when we are in touch with someone, our heart goes out to that person. People with well-balanced heart chakras are in touch with their feelings and nurture themselves and encourage others. An understimulated heart chakra makes a person overly emotional, insecure, sad, and have a strong need to give to others. Most people suffering from codependency have blocked heart chakras. When this chakra is overstimulated, the person will be possessive, controlling, demanding, and jealous.

### Throat Chakra

**Color:** Blue
**Function:** Communication, creativity
**Glands:** Thyroid and parathyroid
**Sense:** Sound
**Desires:** Inner peace
**Keyword:** Concepts

The throat chakra is situated at the level of the throat. It's the chakra of communication and self-expression, especially the spoken word. It seeks the truth in all things and plays a vital role in transmitting thoughts and ideas to the lower four chakras. At an emotional level, the throat chakra enhances idealism, love, and understanding. It provides contentment, peace of mind, and a strong sense of faith. Someone with a well-balanced throat chakra will be kind and considerate of others. This person will speak their mind without any concerns about what others might think. When this chakra is overstimulated, the person will be arrogant, overbearing, and sarcastic. They will enjoy speaking at great length but have no interest in listening to others. When this chakra is blocked or understimulated, the person will be uncommunicative, introverted, weak, fearful, unreliable, and feel a lack of purpose in life.

### Brow Chakra

**Color:** Indigo
**Function:** Intuition, thought, perception
**Glands:** Pituitary
**Sense:** Psychic
**Desires:** To be in harmony with the universe
**Keyword:** Intuition

Often referred to as the third eye, the brow chakra is situated in the center of the forehead just above the eyebrows. This chakra is concerned with psychic and spiritual matters and governs the mind in addition to controlling all the other chakras. At an emotional level, this chakra increases our understanding of the everyday world by making us aware of our spiritual natures. We pick up other people's thoughts, feelings, and intuitions with the brow chakra. When this chakra is overstimulated, the person will be proud, authoritative, devious, and rigid. When understimulated, the person will be timid, hesitant, overwhelmed, unassertive, and prone to tension headaches.

### Crown Chakra

**Color:** Violet

**Function:** Union with the Divine

**Glands:** Pineal

**Sense:** Inner wisdom

**Desires:** Universal understanding

**Keyword:** Spirituality

The crown chakra is situated at the top of the head. Artists often show it as a halo in paintings of a spiritually evolved figure. The crown chakra has the difficult task of balancing and harmonizing the often-conflicting sides of our natures. It also helps us gain insight and understand the interconnectedness of all living things. The crown chakra cannot be activated until all the other chakras have been mastered and are in a state of balance. When it's balanced, this chakra brings enlightenment and a sense of being at one with the entire universe. When this chakra is overstimulated, the person will be angry, depressed, destructive, skeptical, and overly materialistic. The person is likely to suffer from severe headaches. When understimulated, the person will be withdrawn, isolated, remote, lethargic, and feel unable to experience the joys of life.

## Chakra Balancing

Chakra balancing is a form of energy healing that releases emotional blocks that are trapped inside the chakras. People often feel years younger after balancing their chakras as energy flows freely through their bodies giving them the necessary energy, stimulation, motivation, and joy to thoroughly enjoy life.

When doing a chakra balancing for someone else, I like to discuss what I'm doing as I'm doing it. I used to start by asking them if they knew what was causing the negativity but learned that many people are reluctant to discuss these matters and found it best not to pursue it. However, I still mention the most common reasons for negativity to appear in the different chakras.

Emotional factors are the most common cause of blockages in the chakras:

**Root:** Insecurity, self-doubt, and unwillingness to let go of the past

**Sacral:** Selfishness, self-centeredness, and difficulties in communicating well with others

**Solar:** Low self-esteem and feelings of powerlessness.

**Heart:** Difficulties in expressing emotions, holding back, lack of empathy

**Throat:** Frustration caused by lack of verbal skills. Inability to express innermost feelings

**Brow:** Rigidity, stubbornness, and a strong desire to escape into dreams.

**Crown:** Feelings of isolation and alienation from others. Rigid, stubborn outlook

### • • • Exercise 8 • • •

### *How to Balance Your Own Chakras*

In addition to your pendulum, you'll need a pen and paper to record your results.

1. Sit in a straight-backed chair. Close your eyes and take a few deep breaths to relax your body. When you feel ready, open your eyes and pick up your pendulum.
2. Hold your pendulum so the weight is at about the level of your root chakra. Wait, and after a brief period your pendulum will start moving. Notice the size and direction of the pendulum's movement and record it on a piece of paper. At this stage you're gathering information.

3. Repeat the previous step with the other chakras. Ideally, you should receive a similar response from all of them. Any variations indicate potential problems with the particular chakra. If the pendulum doesn't move at all, it's a sign of blockage.
4. After checking all seven chakras, hold your pendulum in front of any chakras that indicated they were not aligned with the others. Swing your pendulum in clockwise circles for about thirty seconds in front of each one while asking your physical body to realign itself.
5. Perform step two again to make sure that all your chakras are in balance. Repeat steps four and two again if necessary.

You'll find that most of the time it's easier to balance someone else's chakras than it is to work on your own. In practice, I usually ask a friend who is interested in pendulum practices to balance mine and then balance theirs in return. This practice is a good and mutually beneficial way for both of you to learn more about chakras as well as the pendulum.

### • • • Exercise 9 • • •
### *How to Balance Other People's Chakras*

You'll be amazed at how positive someone will feel after you've balanced their chakras. After removing a blockage, they'll feel the result immediately. In addition to your friend and your pendulum, you'll need a glass of water. Here's the process:

1. Before you start, tell your pendulum, "I am open to being a channel for healing." Your pendulum should give a positive response to this. You're not ready to perform any healing if you get a negative response. There'll be a reason for this: You might be dehydrated (if you think that's a possibility, drink a glass of water and ask again). However, you might be overtired, stressed, worried, or not feeling well. Take care of whatever could be causing the negative response before trying again.
2. Ask the person to lie on their back and make themselves comfortable.

3. Hold your pendulum over the person's root chakra at the base of the spine and ask: "Is (person's name)'s root chakra in good health?"The pendulum will give a positive or negative answer. Make a note of the response and ask the same question while holding your pendulum over each chakra in turn.
4. If your pendulum gave a positive response to all the questions, congratulate the person—this is extremely rare. Most of the time, you'll continue by finding out which chakra is the most out of balance. Ask your pendulum about all the afflicted chakras in turn: "Is (person's name)'s (name of chakra) the most out of balance?" Continue asking questions until you know which chakras need the most attention.
5. Tell your pendulum that you're going to replace the negative energies with positive energies, and ask it to indicate which movement indicates negative energies and positive ones.

6. Fill a glass of water and place the fingers of your hand that is not holding the pendulum into it.
7. Hold your pendulum over the chakra that is most out of balance and ask your pendulum to remove all the negativity from it. It will start moving in the direction that indicates negative energies. This shows that the pendulum is extracting the negative energies and that they're being drawn into the pendulum, across your shoulders, and down into the glass of water.
8. When the pendulum stops moving in the negative direction, take your fingers out of the water and wash your hands thoroughly with soap and running water. Empty the glass of water and wash it thoroughly before refilling it.
9. Repeat this process with the next most imbalanced chakra and continue until all the negative chakras have been treated.
10. Repeat from step two to make sure that all the negativity has been released and the

chakras are now in balance. Every now and again, you'll find that all the negativity has not been released and will need to go through the process again. The chakras are not in balance until you receive a positive response from each chakra.

11. The final step is to visualize the color green while you deliberately swing the pendulum all over the other person's body in the pendulum's positive direction. Green is a healing color; visualizing the healing passing from the pendulum to your friend in this way is important.
12. Allow your friend to relax for a minute or two before getting up.

You'll find your friend will feel revitalized and full of the joys of life after having their chakras balanced. You'll discover that you'll also feel revitalized after performing the chakra balancing.

## Harmonious Chakras

This is an exercise you can do every day that takes only a few minutes. It will help you keep your chakras well balanced and in harmony.

Copy or write down the following script onto a sheet of paper and suspend your pendulum over it. Swing it in clockwise circles as you read the script, silently or out loud. If you wish, you can change the words to suit your personal needs.

> I ask Divine Spirit (universal life force, God, or whatever name you wish) to guide, guard, and protect me throughout the day, no matter where I am, or what I'm doing. I ask that my personal values, including honesty, integrity, and love, be part of everything I do today, and that I can retain a cheerful and positive outlook in every situation I find myself in.
>
> I also ask that my chakra system remains in perfect balance and harmony all day long, and that this enables me to help and deal kindly with everyone I interact with. I desire the highest good for everyone I encounter.
>
> I ask my pendulum to continue making clockwise circles until my chakras are balanced, all negativity has

left my body, and all fears, doubts, and worries have faded away into nothing. Thank you for all the blessings in my life.

Allow your pendulum to continue circling after you've finished the script to be sure that the ideas you've spoken are accepted and can take hold. Note that it can take from several seconds up to about a minute for this to happen. Once your pendulum changes direction or stops moving, thank it and continue with your day.

## How to Lead a Balanced Life

Many people focus on parts of their lives at the expense of others. I'm sure you've met people who are obsessively focused on making money or spend all their spare time at the gym. I know a man who's a walking encyclopedia. He has several degrees but is unable to carry out a simple conversation in a social setting. You wouldn't describe any of these people as well-balanced.

Here's an exercise devised by well-known American dowser Isidore Friedman. He used his pendulum every month to check how well balanced he was in five areas of his life:

**Physical:** Good health, exercise, food, and clothing.

**Mental:** Intellectual acuity, communication, and sharing of ideas and knowledge.

**Financial:** Earning sufficient income, investments, and good money management.

**Social:** Love, friendships, and getting along well with others.

**Spiritual:** Inner growth and seeking a purpose in life.

In his book, *The Mathematics of Consciousness* he describes drawing a five-pointed star within which he would write down the five areas. In the center of the star, he wrote his name.

To check how he was doing, he would hold his pendulum over each point in turn and ask, "Am I unbalanced in (whatever area of life was indicated)?"

After this, he was able to ask questions about the area or areas that were deficient. If his pendulum indicated that he was deficient in, for instance, the physical area, he would ask questions about exercise, physical fitness, whether to visit his doctor for a checkup, and if he was getting enough sleep. Sometimes two areas were connected. When totally focused on making money, the spiritual aspects of life could fall to neglect. Paying more attention to spirituality could therefore balance both areas at the same time (Friedman 1974, 48).

You'll find it well worth your while to experiment with this exercise. It's helped me, and I know of many other people, several of whom are members of a dowsing society, who have also found it helpful.

A fellow member of a dowsing society I belong to became alarmed when her pendulum told her she was deficient in the physical area. She told me that there was little she could do about it—she'd tried the gym and a number of sports but hadn't found anything she enjoyed doing. I suggested she write a list of activities she thought might be enjoyable and ask her pendulum about each one. It took her weeks to do this, but her pendulum gave positive responses to two items on her list: water aerobics and yoga. Much to her surprise, she found she enjoyed both and is delighted that her pendulum told her to try two activities she would never have considered otherwise.

## How You and Your Pendulum Can Help Your Pets

Most people who have pets consider them part of the family and are distressed when they sense that something is wrong. Many years ago, my wife and I had a Labrador who took himself to the veterinarian whenever he felt unwell. This was, of course, extremely unusual—it fascinated our vet. Obviously if you thought your pet was feeling unwell, you'd be concerned, though it's hard to know if you should seek medical help right away or wait for a while and hope the problem resolves itself.

Fortunately, your pendulum can help. You can hold it over your pet and ask if the problem is serious. If the response is positive, you should take it to a veterinarian right away. If the response is negative, ask your pet if it is suffering pain. Further questions will enable you to find out exactly where the problem is. You may find that the problem is dietary or perhaps your pet has an infection or some other easily solved problem. If your pet is getting older, the problem might be arthritis, and you can dowse further to find out which medication will be the most effective.

It's also possible that your pet might be lacking valuable nutrients in their diet. You can dowse different brands of pet food to see which one is best nutritionally for your pet. You can also do the same thing to find out which brand they like most.

No matter what the problem might be and even when there is no problem, your pet will enjoy receiving healing energy from you. This form of emotional healing balances your pet's chakras in the same way it does with a person.

### • • • Exercise 10 • • •
### *Emotional Healing with Your Pet*

1. Start by spending several minutes cuddling and playing with your pet. Tell your pet how much you love him or her and how much pleasure and joy he or she has brought into your life. Continue talking but gradually reduce the play while continuing to stroke and pat your pet.
2. Continue talking but stop making physical contact. When you stop petting your pet, he or she is likely to look at you as if asking why you've stopped but will then sit or lie down beside you.
3. Tell your pet that you're now going to balance his or her chakras. Hold your pendulum about two inches above the base of your pet's spine and ask your pendulum: "Is (pet's name) root chakra in good health?" Make a note of

the response you get and continue working your way up your pet's spine asking about each of the chakras in turn.

4. Once you've done that, hold your pendulum over the chakras that need work and ask your pendulum to remove all the negativity that's present in the affected chakras. Your pendulum will start moving and won't stop until the negative energy has gone.
5. Wash your hands thoroughly after this. Finally, check your pet's chakras again and if necessary, repeat step four over any chakras that have not fully returned to balance.
6. Once the chakras are in balance, wash your hands again and cleanse your pendulum.

. . . ( . . .

You can check your pet's chakras even when they're not with you. Suspend your pendulum and ask about the health of each chakra in turn. Continue by removing the negativity and then check the chakras again.

You can also send healing energy to your companion by swinging your pendulum in clockwise circles over your pet while mentally sending thoughts of love and healing to it.

### • • • Exercise 11 • • •
### *How to Establish a Psychic Connection with Your Pet*

Most pet owners believe that they communicate with their pets. You can take this a great deal further with the help of your pendulum.

1. Spend several minutes petting and playing with your pet. Talk to them while doing this.
2. Gradually slow down the amount of petting and cuddling until you stop making physical contact. Continue talking. Your pet might appear surprised when you stop stroking them but will sit or lie down next to you.
3. Pick up your pendulum and mentally tell your pet how much you love them. Mentally ask your pet if they can "hear" you. If your pendulum gives a positive response, you'll know that your pet has heard you, and you can move on to the next step. If you get a negative response or no response at all,

swing your pendulum over your pet in a clockwise direction and, while it is spinning, mentally tell your pet how much you love them, and think of happy times you've spent together. Tell your pet that you're hoping the pendulum will help bring you even closer to each other. When the pendulum stops moving say "thank you" three times.

4. Pause for several seconds and then ask your pet if he or she can hear you. It doesn't matter at this stage if you get another negative response. You are trying something new, and your pet might be puzzled as to what you're trying to do. Spin your pendulum clockwise again and send your pet thoughts of love until it stops. As it stops, say "I love you."
5. When the pendulum stops moving silently say "thank you" three times. Wait for about sixty seconds as your pet may have worked out what you're trying to do and could respond. If that happens, you can start asking questions. If nothing happens, put

your pendulum aside for a day or two and then try again.

. . . ☾ . . .

Once your pet has given a positive response, you can start asking as many questions as you wish. Be aware that pets can lie and even ignore questions they don't want to respond to. When your pet stops responding, you'll know it's time to finish the session. Mentally say, "I understand. We'll talk again soon. Remember, I love you."

In the next chapter we'll explore many ways you can enhance your life by using your pendulum in your home and garden.

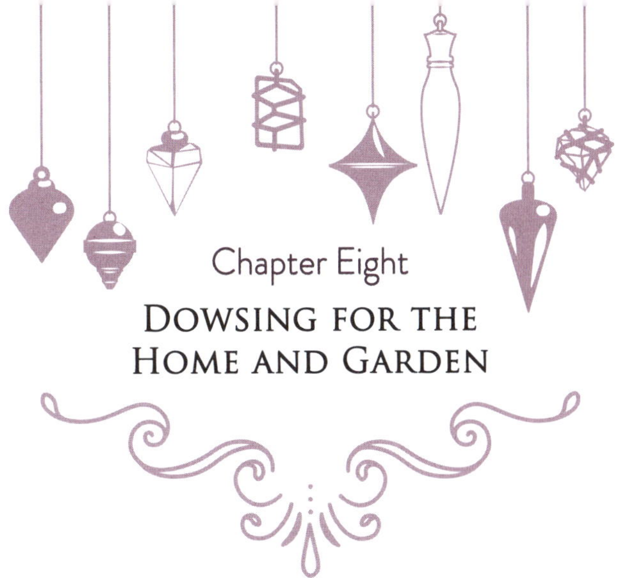

# Chapter Eight

# Dowsing for the Home and Garden

A home is much more than somewhere to live. It has many powerful associations, ideally a place of security where you feel safe, comfortable, and happy. It's a place where you feel welcome and loved by your friends and family. When you're at home you should be able to laugh, express yourself freely, and be yourself. It's also a sanctuary where you feel protected, supported, and safe physically and emotionally.

Every time you do something pleasant and enjoyable in your home, you build up positive energy. Singing, dancing, cooking, reading, and working on a hobby are good examples. Meditation, prayer, and other spiritual activities are good ways to increase the home's energy. Making love, exercising, and relaxing in a bubble bath are other examples.

A lady I know watches television by candlelight, instead of having the house lights on. She loves candles and after a difficult marriage breakup found them healing, nurturing, and relaxing. Visitors always comment on the positive energy they feel in her home.

All the people living in the home also create a mixture of positive and negative energy that affects the quality of the environment.

Unfortunately, there are other factors that adversely affect the quality of home and family life. Negative thoughts and emotions, sadness, arguments, abuse, and domestic violence create negative energy that builds up in the home over time. Fears, doubts, worries, hate, and anger all create toxic negativity that robs the home of energy and joy.

If you're renting a home, it may still contain negative energies left by the previous occupants and even more so if you rent a furnished property, as negativity can linger in the furniture. Whenever you feel any negativity in your surroundings, be it at home, work, or anywhere else, you can release it with your pendulum.

I know many people who give their homes energy cleansings once a year, usually on New Year's Day. However, you can energy cleanse your house whenever you wish. The process is straightforward and enjoyable to perform.

Start, in the usual way, by protecting yourself, and ask the "Can I?", "Should I?", and "May I?" questions. Drink a glass of water.

Once you've done that, stand somewhere in the middle of the house and ask your pendulum if this is a good time to give your home an energy cleanse. Proceed only if you receive a positive response. There's no point in continuing if the response is negative. Put your pendulum away and ask the question again a week or two later.

If your pendulum gives you a positive response, go to the first room you want to cleanse. Stand in the middle of the room and sense the energy around you. You may find it helpful to close your eyes while doing this. Open your eyes, think about your need to rid the room of negative energy, and swing your pendulum counterclockwise for sixty seconds.

Stop the movement of the pendulum and ask it three questions: "Has all the negative emotional energy been dispelled and removed?" "Has all the negative mental energy been dispelled and removed?" "Has all the negative spiritual energy been dispelled and removed?" If you receive a negative response to any of these questions, swing the pendulum counterclockwise again for sixty seconds while focusing on your need to totally remove the negative energy that has resisted removal.

Once you've received a positive response to all three questions swing the pendulum clockwise for sixty seconds while focusing on filling the room with positive energy. Stop the pendulum's movement after sixty seconds and ask your pendulum if the room is now filled with positive energy. Repeat this as many times as necessary to ensure the room contains nothing but positive energy.

You can now repeat the process in every room of the house, including attics, basements, hallways, walk-in closets, and storage areas.

After cleansing every part of the house, stand in a position near the center of the house. Swing the pendulum clockwise for sixty seconds while silently or out loud repeating: "May this house be filled with love."

Pause for a few seconds and then ask your pendulum if the house is now full of love. Most homes need more than sixty seconds to fill with love, so you'll probably have to repeat this a number of times until you receive a positive response.

If you experience any problems during the cleansing, remove any clutter in the room and try again. If the problem persists, swing your pendulum counterclockwise in each corner of the room, where negative energies frequently collect.

There are many ways you can use your pendulum to help with everyday household matters. For instance, you can ask your pendulum for the perfect place to hang a painting, put up a shelf, or advise where a specific piece of furniture should go. You can hold your pendulum over the different colors in paint charts to find out which colors would be best when redecorating.

Your pendulum can advise you on the best place in your bedroom for your bed. Changing the position of the bed might be all that's required to give you a good night's sleep.

## How to Ask about the Health of Your Garden and Plants

- Are any pests or diseases adversely affecting my plants?
- Do I need to add fertilizer or nutrients to the soil?
- Do any plants need immediate attention?
- Does this plant need more/less water?
- Is this plant thriving in this location?
- Is (specific location in garden) suitable for (specific plant)?
- Should I prune or trim this plant?
- Will this plant thrive in my garden?
- Will this plant get on well with my other plants?
- Is this plant free from pests or diseases?
- Does this plant need full sun, partial shade, or full shade?
- Is this the right time to buy this plant?

You can test your bed by holding your pendulum over it and asking if it's in the right place in the room.

If you've moved into a new area, you can ask your pendulum to help you find a good doctor, dentist, veterinarian, school, and even work opportunities. You do this by making a list of the different possibilities and holding your pendulum over each one in turn while asking questions. If you're looking for a doctor, for instance, you can start by thinking of your family's needs and asking about those particular requirements. You might want a doctor who is friendly, willing to listen, and knowledgeable about your family's specific health concerns. Or perhaps you want a doctor in a smaller clinic as opposed to a larger, busier hospital, or one whose office is closer to your office or home.

## The Pendulum and Your Garden

Many years ago, I spoke at a gardening club and was delighted to learn that several of the members used a pendulum to help them look after their plants. You can use your pendulum to advise you where to set up a vegetable garden or a specific plant. Even if you don't have a garden, you can use a pendulum to ensure the health of a potted plant. You can ask your pendulum which plant or plants to buy for a specific location. It will also tell you how much compost and fertilizer a particular plant or garden needs.

If you buy a new plant and are not sure where to place it in your garden, hold your pendulum over it and ask it questions. You might ask if you should plant it right away. If not, when should you plant it? You could ask where the best place in your garden for it would be. You can ask further questions about the soil, drainage, amount of direct sunlight, and the size and depth of the hole that would need to be dug. I've learned the hard way that it's best to plant the new purchase where the pendulum suggests rather than any other position you had in mind.

Thousands of years ago, farmers learned that some plants grow better in close proximity to some plants but failed to flourish when planted close to others. Tomatoes and potatoes don't do well together, for instance, but tomatoes and basil thrive when planted close to each other, as do potatoes and beans. This concept is known as companion gardening, when two or more plants are deliberately grown close together to help them both grow better.

Your pendulum will tell you how compatible your new purchase will be with any other plant in your garden. You can easily do this by holding your pendulum over the two plants individually and asking them if they'd be happy together. If they are, your pendulum will respond positively to each one. Another method is to place the two plants about two feet apart and hold your pendulum between them. The two plants are compatible if your pendulum swings to and fro between them. This is a particularly useful thing to do with potted plants, as it's easy to place the compatible plants together and keep them well away from any incompatible plants.

You can determine the health of a plant by holding your pendulum over it and asking questions. If it's unwell, your pendulum will give a negative response. Send positive messages of good health and vitality to the plant silently or out loud. Your pendulum may start giving a positive response while you're doing this. This means you've resolved the problem. If this doesn't happen, you can ask further questions to find out what the problem is and what you need to do to resolve it.

By learning how to use a pendulum you've already started a program of self-improvement. The next chapter looks at ways your pendulum can enhance your life by removing long-held negative beliefs, increasing motivation, improving relationships, helping you progress in your career, and discovering what you want to do with your life.

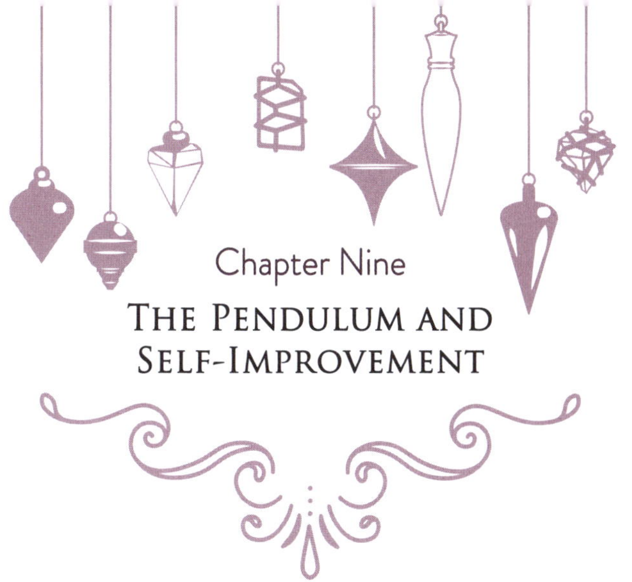

# Chapter Nine
# The Pendulum and Self-Improvement

Your pendulum is a powerful tool that can guide and help you in many areas of your life, including your sense of confidence, motivation, and the release of subconscious blocks.

About twenty years ago, a neighbor asked me if I could help his daughter, an attractive woman in her early twenties who had never had a romantic relationship. Her problem was that she was painfully shy and found it hard to talk with people she didn't know well. Fortunately, I was able to show her how to use a pendulum to resolve her problems, and today she is happily married with two teenage children.

You can use your pendulum in the same way to provide guidance and help in every area of your life. If you're looking for a new hobby, you could ask your pendulum about a variety of potential interests and find out which of them you'd enjoy the most. If someone recommends a movie, your pendulum will tell you if you'd enjoy it too. Your pendulum will be happy to advise you where to go on your summer vacation. Your pendulum can provide advice on exercise, your clothing, the best food for you to eat, what clubs to join, the best teacher or tutor for anything you want to learn, and much more.

Your pendulum can also give you advice on what to turn down or avoid. A friend of mine is a qualified doctor but works full-time as a magician. He never wanted to be a doctor, but his father and grandfather were both doctors so it was expected that he would become one too. Many people set goals to please others and almost invariably pay a heavy price for it. My friend wasn't strong enough to tell his parents that he wanted to follow his own dream rather than theirs and spent many unhappy years studying for a career he never wanted. If he'd had a pendulum before starting college, it would have told him that he was going in the wrong direction and may have suggested he studied theater rather than medicine. Fortunately, he changed careers and today is both happy and successful. My former dentist spent his whole life in a career he loathed as he was never brave enough to pursue his dream of being a professional photographer. It's sad to think how many people are caught in a trap of their own making.

Fortunately, with the help of your pendulum, you'll be able to choose goals that are right for you.

## Know Yourself

The famous saying, "Know yourself" was inscribed above the entrance to the Temple of Apollo at Delphi. It's vitally important to understand your own personality traits, psychological disposition, nature, and capabilities. You need to be aware of your particular skills, talents, and motivations to decide what you want to do with your life. If you're not naturally athletic, for example, you'll struggle to become a successful footballer. If you're painfully shy and easily hurt, politics would not be a natural choice of career.

You also want to be realistic about what you're capable of achieving. Many people dream of becoming a famous actor or singer without realizing how much talent and hard work, not to mention luck, is involved. Of course, some people do the opposite and achieve less than they can, simply because they doubt their abilities. Your pendulum is a useful tool for knowing yourself and setting goals that are realistic and achievable.

## Self-Assessment

As your pendulum enables you to receive answers from your subconscious mind, you can ask it any questions about yourself, your character, goals, hopes, dreams, and anything else.

Here's an interesting self-assessment exercise that can indicate areas of your life that need to be worked on. You may not be happy with the answers your pendulum provides. However, it will give you plenty of food for thought and might motivate you to make necessary changes in your life.

### • • • Exercise 12 • • •
### *Self-Assessment*

Start by making a list of positive statements that you already have or would like to possess. Here are some examples:

- I am happy.
- I am loved.
- I am a good person.
- I am successful.
- I am good with money.
- I enjoy excellent health.
- I am confident.
- I achieve my goals.
- I am enthusiastic.
- I attract good things to me.
- I am following my heart's desire.

Add as many other statements to this list as you wish. If you hold a responsible position with staff to look after, you might write, "I am a good boss." You could add, "I am happily married," or "I am a caring parent," if those statements applied to you.

1. Sit down somewhere where you're unlikely to be interrupted and hold your pendulum while saying each of the statements out loud. Pause after saying each one and wait to see what response your pendulum makes. It will move in a positive direction

if your subconscious mind agrees with the statement. It will give a negative response if it disagrees with what you're saying and will not move at all if it has no particular view on what you said.

2. Record your results. It may be difficult, but don't question the findings until your pendulum has responded to each statement.
3. Once you've finished, look at the statements that received a negative response. Some of them won't surprise you. If you're currently unwell, you won't be surprised to receive a negative response to "I enjoy excellent health." However, some may surprise you. You might have thought you were reasonably happy but your subconscious mind disagreed and indicated otherwise.
4. Ask your pendulum further questions to find out why it gave a negative response to certain statements. Once you know the reasons, you can take action to resolve whatever the difficulties happen to be. Be

kind and compassionate to yourself while doing this.

5. Keep your responses and repeat this exercise regularly to give you feedback on how you're progressing.
6. Add other statements to the list as they occur to you.

## Lifelong Learning

Nowadays, it's easier to access information on virtually any subject at all than ever before. Millions of books are published every year, and the amount of content available online is increasing by the day. The quantity of information can be overwhelming, making it hard to find exactly what you want. Fortunately, your pendulum can provide advice on what to investigate and what to ignore. Another problem when researching online is to determine how correct the information you are reading is. Anyone can post almost anything they want online, so the chances are high that at least some of what you come across is misleading or even deliberately wrong. Most of this can be avoided by asking your pendulum, "Is this information true?" and "Is this claim correct?"

Because of the potential problems of information overload and misinformation, I do most of my research using published books. I realize they can also be inaccurate, but if they've been published by a reputable publisher, they'll have been properly edited and the facts checked before publication. Most serious books also contain references to where their authors obtained the information, and I enjoy checking out these sources.

You can also use your pendulum to let you know which books to buy and which to put back on the shelves. I ask my pendulum if a particular book will be useful to me and, when I get a positive response, ask further questions to ensure that I'm purchasing the right book. If I find my pendulum recommends two books, I ask which one will be more useful to me now. Sometimes my pendulum insists that I need both; when that occurs, I usually buy them. However, if I need only one of them immediately, I may ask which one I should buy today.

## Confidence

When I worked as a hypnotherapist, I regularly helped people with confidence issues. At times it seemed as if almost everyone needed more confidence. In fact, everyone is confident in some areas of their lives but lacks it in others. If you've been doing the same type of work for some years, you'll feel confident that you can do everything necessary to do a good job. However, you may feel a lack of confidence when it comes to meeting new people and making friends, and in fact most people are. A client of mine was a successful CEO who could stand on stage in an auditorium and deliver a powerful speech but was unable to enter a room full of people on her own. Fortunately, I was able to help her resolve that problem.

Confident people believe in their abilities and judgment. They're able to act, make decisions, and face challenges without fears, doubts, or worries. They bounce back quickly after setbacks because they feel good about themselves and know they will ultimately succeed.

You may not need to develop the skill to speak publicly if that's not expected of you as part of your job, for example, but fortunately confidence is a skill that anyone can develop.

### • • • Exercise 13 • • •

### *How to Develop Confidence*

1. Sit down in a comfortable chair. Make sure that the elbow of the arm holding your

pendulum is resting on an armrest or some other support. Close your eyes.

2. Think about a time when you felt relaxed and happy. Smile as you recollect these happy memories.
3. Think about something you're good at or a time when someone acknowledged you for something you did. Smile again.
4. After steps two and three have helped you relax and you feel ready, think about something you're going to be doing in the near future that you don't feel confident about. Chances are you'll immediately start thinking negatively about whatever it is, perhaps imagining all the ways it could go wrong. As soon as you become aware that this is what you're doing, stop visualizing. If necessary, picture a large red X to indicate that particular line of thinking is forbidden.
5. In your mind's eye, see yourself doing whatever it happens to be in a calm and relaxed manner. Visualize yourself smiling and laughing with friends and/or colleagues

as you perform the task. See yourself after you've performed it feeling relaxed and happy. Tell yourself, "This is how it's going to be from now on." Allow a sense of pride and pleasure to sweep over you as you know that you'll always feel confident performing this task in the future.

6. Repeat step 4 three times.
7. Open your eyes and look at your pendulum. It will probably indicate your positive response. If it's not moving, wait several seconds to give it time to respond. There's a slight possibility that it will react negatively to what you've just done. There's no need to be concerned—it simply means it hasn't accepted the new confident you yet.
8. Repeat this exercise at least once a day. In addition to that, you can also use your pendulum to increase the effectiveness of it. Two or three times a day (more if you have time), deliberately swing your pendulum in your positive direction and repeat step 5 in your mind while watching it.

9. When you start feeling a sense of pride and satisfaction in your mind as soon as you reach step 5, step out of your comfort zone and do whatever it happens to be. Your confidence will increase each time you do this.

## Motivation

Motivation is the desire to achieve a particular goal. The goal can be anything at all, as simple as making sure you get to work on time or something highly involved that will take a great deal of time, such as designing a large building project. Many people spend years working hard to earn a college degree. Others spend countless hours training at a sport in the hope of becoming a top athlete. Without motivation, none of these people would achieve these goals. When I worked in publishing in London many years ago, I went to a cocktail party to honor several well-known authors. I was surprised when the publisher who was hosting the event told me that within five miles of where we were, there were many better writers than the ones he was honoring at the party. "The difference," he told me, "is that the authors in this room write. The others only think about writing." He was basically saying that the authors in the room were motivated to write while the others weren't.

We're all motivated to perform enjoyable tasks but find it hard to get motivated to do something less appealing, such as a minor household repair or tidying up a messy garage. It's especially hard to get motivated to do something we don't want to do, such as apologizing for something we did (or didn't) do. Fortunately, your pendulum can help you gain the motivation you require whenever you need it.

The first step is to identify why you need to perform a particular task. If the task is to hang up some pictures, the why could be to beautify your home or to please your partner. If you're planning to become a dentist, you need to go to college for many years. The why is to gain the qualifications you need.

Hold your pendulum and tell it what you need motivation for. Explain why you want to achieve this goal and ask your pendulum if it will help you. It should respond by moving to indicate your positive response. If it doesn't, it's a sign that your why isn't strong enough. In this case, you'll need to think more deeply about your long-term goals and what you want to achieve.

Once your pendulum has responded positively, you can deliberately swing your pendulum in your positive direction while thinking about your goal and the benefits that will come your way once you've accomplished it. If the goal is a long-term one, you might reward yourself in some way at different stages of the project.

The final stage is to hold your pendulum while telling yourself that you're going to start work on the goal immediately. When your pendulum gives your positive response get up and start as quickly as you can.

## Decision Making

Like everyone else, you probably find it hard to make decisions at times. You might delay making it for a day or two while thinking about all the pros and cons that are involved. While doing this, you're likely to get confused and agonize over the decision you have to make. Overthinking makes matters worse.

Minor decisions can be just as hard to make as major ones. Choosing what dress to wear for a social occasion is sometimes no less crippling than deciding whether or not to accept a new job offer. Fear of making the wrong decision is one of the reasons for this.

## How to Make Your Self-Improvement Goals More Effective

Set your intentions as clearly as possible before dowsing. It can be helpful to write down your intention before picking up your pendulum.

Start a morning ritual with your pendulum and ask it a single question relating to self-improvement. For example: "Am I aligned with my goal of (whatever you are working on)?"

Regularly ask: "Am I holding onto limiting self-beliefs?" If you get a positive answer, ask further questions to identify it. From there, eliminate whatever it is with the help of your pendulum.

Whenever you feel uncertain about anything, ask your pendulum if the doubt is based on reality or fear. This will clarify your feelings, letting you act on the answer or ask further questions before proceeding.

Ask your pendulum questions while you're saying affirmations or visualizing your goals. You might, for instance, ask it: "Is my confidence increasing every day?"

The solution to indecision is your pendulum. After all, it makes decisions every time it gives you an answer. Remember that it does this by tapping into your subconscious mind—it therefore will give you the response that will be most helpful. That said, if you have an emotional interest in an outcome, it's best to ask someone who has no vested interest to use the pendulum for you.

After receiving your pendulum's response, you can confirm it by asking, "Is this the truth?"

## Affirmations and Your Pendulum

No one knows how many thoughts we have every day, but many experts guess it's between fifty and sixty thousand. Of course, many of these thoughts are the same thoughts we thought yesterday, the day before, and maybe even years before. Consequently, the number of new thoughts we have every day is much lower than sixty thousand. More important than the total number of thoughts is the number of positive thoughts we have compared to the number of negative ones. It's vitally important to our well-being to think more positive thoughts than negative ones—most of us are undermining ourselves every day with our own negative thoughts. And one good way to ensure we're having more positive thoughts than negative ones is the practice of affirmations. These are positive statements always framed in the present tense and said firmly, with conviction, as if you already have the desired quality of the particular affirmation. They are always spoken enthusiastically and repeated over and over again until the subconscious mind accepts them and they become a natural part of your life. Here are some examples:

- I am enthusiastic and positive.
- I am confident and believe in myself.
- I have everything I need to achieve success.
- I am grateful for all the blessings in my life.
- I choose to be kind.
- I deserve to be rich.
- I love others and others love me.
- Day by day, in every way, I'm getting better and better.

You can create affirmations about anything you wish. If you want to lose weight, find the right partner, obtain the right job, enjoy good health, increase your income, or become more successful in life, you can write an affirmation to help you accomplish it. My preference is to write my own, but it's easy to find affirmations online.

The advantage of writing your own is that you can make them exactly right for you and your needs.

Once you've written or chosen an affirmation, you can test it with your pendulum. Hold your pendulum over the written words and say the affirmation out loud. If you receive a positive response, you can start using the affirmation as it is. If you get a negative response, you'll need to change the affirmation or ask further questions to find out why your subconscious mind is rejecting it.

If you're affirming that you deserve love and happiness, it can be disturbing if your pendulum gives a negative response. Your pendulum is effectively telling you that you don't believe in what you're affirming. Maybe you did something you're ashamed of in the past and feel that you don't deserve to be loved. You might have been bullied or treated badly by someone you cared for deeply. There could be any number of reasons why your pendulum responded the way it did.

If you receive this kind of response, you could change the wording or rewrite the affirmation. Alternatively, you could repeat it without using your pendulum as often as you can for two or three days. After this, sit down quietly with your pendulum, close your eyes, and repeat the affirmation ten times. Say the words as enthusiastically as you can and emphasize a different word each time you say it. Open your eyes and see what movement your pendulum is giving you. When your subconscious mind has accepted the affirmation, your pendulum will give a positive response. If not, repeat this until your subconscious mind accepts it.

### • • • Exercise 14 • • •
### *How to Choose the Right Affirmations*

1. Start by writing down several affirmations on individual slips of paper. They should all be relevant to you and your needs.
2. Hold your pendulum over one of them and ask: "Is this a good affirmation for me to use at this time?" Move on to step 3 if your pendulum gives a positive response to the first affirmation. If you get a negative response, suspend your pendulum over each affirmation in turn until you get a positive response.
3. Hold your pendulum over the affirmation that produced a positive response and ask: "Are there any blocks in my mind, body, or spirit that will prevent my subconscious

mind from accepting this affirmation?" If you receive a positive response that there are not, you can move on to step 4. If blocks are indicated, ask further questions to discover what the problem is. Most likely it will be be an old, outmoded belief that needs removing.

4. Ask your pendulum: "Will my subconscious mind accept this affirmation and make it real?" If you receive a positive response, you can start using the affirmation right away. If you receive a negative response, you'll need to ask further questions to discover why your subconscious mind is not accepting it.
5. Say the affirmation out loud and see if your pendulum responds positively to it. This is the most likely response. If you get a negative response, you'll have to repeat steps two through four again to eliminate whatever is causing the problem.
6. Swing your pendulum in a clockwise direction and repeat the affirmation until the pendulum stops. You can do this in a

variety of ways. If other people are near, you might like to do it silently. Whenever possible, I like to say my affirmations out loud to engage my sense of sound in the mix. Use as much energy as possible when saying your affirmations. You might like to say them in different voices, sing them, or place the emphasis on a different word each time you say it.

7. When your pendulum stops moving, say: "Thank you, Divine Spirit. Thank you. Thank you. Thank you."

Repeat the affirmation as often as possible. You might say it silently while waiting in line or traveling on public transport. You can say it in the shower, and while lying in bed. You might say it while looking at yourself in a mirror. At least once a day, repeat step 6. Continue doing this until the contents of the affirmation have been completely absorbed by your subconscious mind and you're demonstrating whatever the affirmation is in your everyday life.

Another good way to use your affirmation is to write it on a card and carry it everywhere with you. Whenever you have a spare moment, look at the words and silently say the affirmation to yourself.

## How to Remove Negative Beliefs and Blocks

Everyone hangs on to at least one negative belief. Most people have a number of them, and some unfortunate people have minds full of painful and negative feelings. Most of these are likely to date back to early childhood experiences and may have served a purpose back then. However, these kinds of beliefs severely limit and harm us when we consciously or unconsciously accept them as the truth as adults.

Have you ever said to yourself: "I'm stupid," "I'm hopeless at math," "I'm weak," "I don't deserve to be rich," and other negative put-downs? If so, they were probably caused by negative subconscious beliefs. False beliefs about money are extremely common and are often caused by parents who tell their children: "We can't afford that," "money doesn't grow on trees," "money is the root of all evil," "it's hard to make money," and other negative remarks about money.

All of these and many others are negative affirmations that lurk in people's subconscious minds, ready and waiting to sabotage them at every opportunity. This is why so many people work hard at something and, just when they're about to succeed, they somehow sabotage themselves and end up in a worse position than before they started. It's sad to think about the countless numbers of people around the world who think they're not good enough and consequently fail to achieve their dreams all because of their own negative thoughts. Fortunately, your pendulum is ready and willing to help you remove these limiting beliefs that hinder and block you at every turn.

### • • • Exercise 15 • • •
### *How to Remove Negative Beliefs*

1. Start by writing a list of everything that's important to you. It makes no difference how long or short your list is or what words you use as long as they're important to you. It's perfectly valid to write "love, home, family, and health" as it is to list "wealth, fame, success, home, love, creativity, travel, health, knowledge, music, friendship, fine wine, sport, and exercise."

2. Hold your pendulum over the first item on your list and ask: "Do I have any subconscious fears or beliefs about (the word)?" If your pendulum gives a negative response, move on to the second item on your list.
3. If your pendulum gives a positive response, you can ask further questions to find out what the negative fears and beliefs are. If the negative belief happened to be about money, for instance, you could ask if it came from your parents. If it didn't, was it caused by something that occurred later, such as a failed investment or business venture? It can be helpful to ask your pendulum about common limiting beliefs about money to see if any of them apply to you. You might ask: "Does my subconscious mind believe I'm not good enough to be wealthy?" "Do I believe I'm not smart enough to make money?" "Will I ever have enough money to enjoy life?" and "Will I achieve success in the field I'm in now?"

4. Continue asking questions until you have a clear idea about what is causing the problem. Once you know what it is, the next step is to eliminate it. However, you can't simply eliminate it—that will cause a vacuum. You need to also instill a new belief opposite to the old one. In this example using money, you need to create a new belief that says you deserve to be rich.
5. Spin your pendulum counterclockwise and ask it to eliminate the unwanted, limiting belief. You might say, preferably out loud:

   I ask Divine Spirit to totally remove all the false thoughts and beliefs I've had about money and how bad it is. I know now that money is just money. It's neither good nor bad, and I have just as much right to abundance as anyone else. I've spent more than enough time holding on to this destructive limiting belief that holds me back and prevents me from showing the world what I'm capable of achieving. I let go of all my old thoughts and beliefs about money, and ask Divine Spirit to help me to totally, completely, and irrevocably eliminate each and every one of them. Thank you. Thank you. Thank you.

Continue talking in this vein until your pendulum stops moving. Pause and relax for a minute or two before going on to the next step. You might drink a glass of water and eat some nuts and raisins before continuing.

6. When you feel ready, swing your pendulum clockwise to instill the positive beliefs about money that you're going to place into your mind, body, and spirit. You might say:

   I thank Divine Spirit for removing all my negative thoughts and beliefs about money, especially my belief that I don't deserve to be rich. I realize now that I deserve just as many of the good things of life as anyone else, and I ask you to help me achieve this goal by filling every cell of my body with positive thoughts and beliefs about money and abundance. Please help me develop a positive prosperity consciousness that will attract money to me. Please encourage me to believe in myself more and more every day. I deserve to be rich in every sense of the word. Thank you for blessing my life with prosperity, abundance, and success. Thank you. Thank you. Thank you.

Continue talking along these lines until your pendulum stops moving.

Some people prefer to perform this exercise without spending time discovering the underlying causes of the problem. If you would prefer to do it that way, eliminate step 3, especially when repeating the exercise.

After doing this exercise once, wait a few days and then test yourself again. Repeat this exercise as many times as necessary to eliminate all your negative programming and beliefs relating to the particular problem.

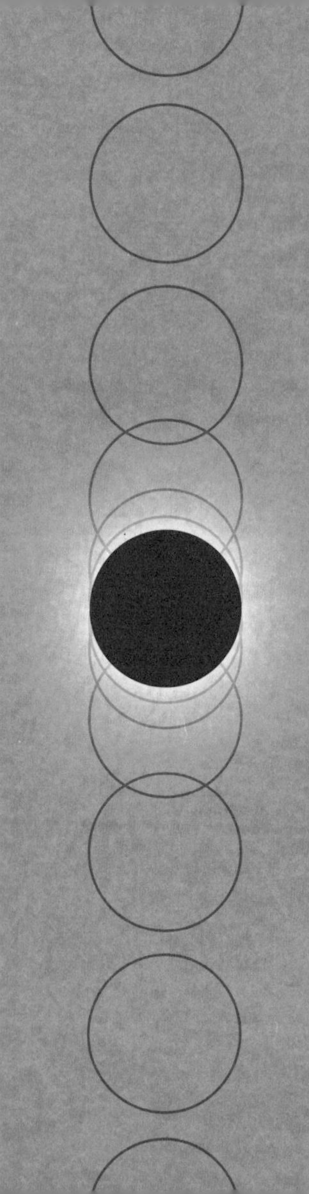

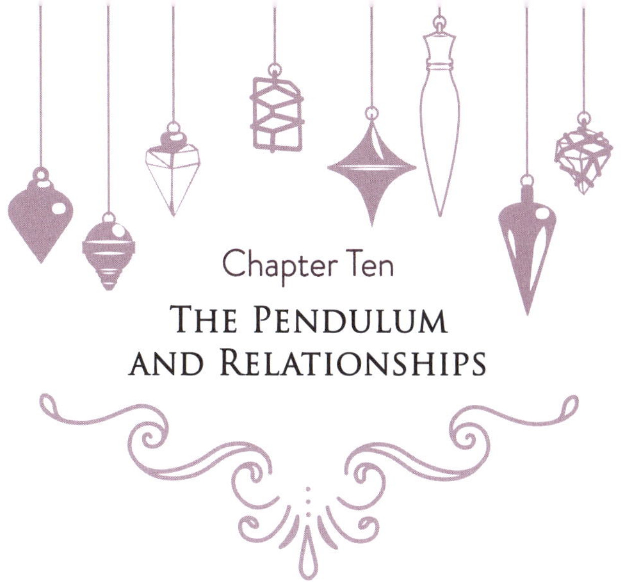

# Chapter Ten
# The Pendulum and Relationships

The relationships we form with others play a vital role in ensuring a happy and fulfilled life. Our emotional and mental well-being is enhanced enormously with good strong relationships with others. People with good social connections are happier, healthier, suffer less stress, and live longer than people who lack companionship. They also gain encouragement, and a sense of purpose from the people they're close to. The happiest people have a network of relationships including romance, family, friendships, work colleagues, and acquaintances.

Some of the most important factors in good relationships are mutual trust, respect, support, love, kindness, commitment, and good communication. People in healthy relationships listen to each other and communicate without judgment. They make time for each other and show interest and concern in their lives.

Your pendulum can provide help and advice on any matters relating to relationships, such as starting a new relationship, enhancing an existing relationship, resolving difficulties and problems, and even ending a relationship that isn't working as smoothly as it should be.

## How to Find the Right Person Online

As life becomes increasingly busy for many people, online dating sites have become an extremely popular way to meet potential partners. Before swiping to express interest, you can hold your pendulum over a photograph or name and ask questions about the person and his or her personality.

If you're not interested in going online to meet someone you can ask your pendulum when you'll meet the right person. You can also ask questions about someone you're going to meet in person. If someone asks you out, your pendulum can tell you whether to accept the invitation. And if the relationship develops you can ask further questions, such as, "Are we compatible?" and "Does (name of person) love me?"

You can learn more about your compatibility with someone else by using your pendulum to assess the other person's mental, physical, emotional, and spiritual compatibility with you. Naturally, it's an extremely good sign if there is compatibility on all four levels. Physical compatibility is a sign that you'd get on well sexually. There's a strong possibility of a good, loving relationship if there's a strong emotional compatibility as well. If you are compatible mentally, physically, and emotionally, the potential for a long-lasting relationship is strong and made even stronger if you two share spiritual compatibility as well. Of course, if the relationship doesn't seem to be going anywhere, your pendulum can also give you advice on whether to end it.

## How to Send Love to Others

You can help many people by sending love to them with your pendulum. All you need to do is to sit down somewhere quiet, spin your pendulum clockwise, and send loving thoughts to the person you have in mind. Continue sending loving thoughts until the pendulum stops.

You can send love to anyone you wish. It could be a stranger you passed on the street, the barista at your local coffee shop, your doctor, your boss, members of your family, or anyone else alive or dead.

You can use your pendulum to send love, forgiveness, and healing to anyone you wish. If someone close to you lives far away or is temporarily away from home, you can send them love as often as you wish. Frequently you'll find that this person will let you know they were thinking of you at the exact moment you were sending them love. If someone has hurt or offended you, you can send them a message of forgiveness, love, and reconciliation. This might start a process that gradually heals the relationship. Even if the relationship is irreparably broken, sending love and forgiveness to the other person always helps you release unnecessary baggage and frees you from all the pain and hurt between you.

### • • • Exercise 16 • • •
### *How to Send Love to Others*

Whenever possible, I perform this exercise in my sacred space and frequently light a white candle (or a green candle if I'm sending healing energy) before starting the ritual.

1. Think of the person you want to communicate with, picturing them in your mind and recalling some happy activities you've done together in the past. Think of your intent in performing the ritual.
2. Spin your pendulum clockwise and talk, preferably out loud, to the person you're contacting. Speak in a conversational manner and tell them everything you want to say. If it's a family member, for instance, you might include updates on other members of the family.
3. The pendulum may (or may not) have stopped spinning while you were talking. Swing it again in a clockwise direction and visualize your message of love (or healing, or forgiveness) flowing from you and being instantly received by the other person. Continue sending positive thoughts until your pendulum stops moving.

## Relationship Dowsing

Your pendulum is a guidance tool, and you need to be careful about the questions you ask. Loving relationships develop naturally, and pendulum dowsing should encourage your choices. You should never invade other people's privacy with your questions. Instead of asking, "Does (person's name) love me?", you could ask: "Should I explore a deeper connection with (person's name)?" You can't ask: "Can I make (person's name) fall in love with me?" This is manipulative and ignores the fact that both you and the other person have free will. Love should develop naturally.

Fortunately, there are many positive questions you can ask, such as: "Is this relationship aligned with my highest good?" "Should I continue investing time and effort into this relationship?" "Should I focus on self-healing before thinking about a new relationship?" "Is the time right for me to commit to a romantic relationship?"

Remember to use your intuition as well as your pendulum. Your pendulum can guide and help you but should be used in conjunction with your own feelings and inner knowing.

4. Send a blessing to the person you're communicating with while visualizing the person in your mind as clearly as you can.
5. When your mental picture of the person starts to fade, say a prayer of thanks to the Divine for enabling you and the other person to communicate with each other in this way.

. . . ☾ . . .

It can be particularly helpful to send love to people you don't like. If you do this for any length of time, you'll find yourself getting on better with them. They won't have any idea what you're doing but will subliminally pick up and respond to your loving feelings.

You don't have to send love to one person at a time—you could also send love to all your friends on social media or all the patients in a hospital, for instance. And there's no reason why you can't send love to all humanity. While doing this, don't forget to send love to your favorite pet or other animals. You can send love to all the plants in your garden. You can send love to your spirit guides and angel guardians.

It's also vitally important to send love to yourself. You'll appreciate yourself more as a result, and your relationships with everyone you interact with will improve. Your self-esteem will grow, and you'll be able to withstand all the problems and difficulties that come your way.

You can also bless others when you send love to them. People often think that they need to be religious or spiritually evolved to perform a blessing but you don't need to be a member of the clergy or belong to any religion to do it. Pagans frequently say "blessed be," as one example. In fact, you may have blessed many people over the years. Have you ever said "Bless you" to someone after they sneezed? A simple smile to someone who needs it is a type of blessing, just as is asking someone how they are, as long as you ask it with genuine interest. Wishing someone good luck is a form of blessing. In the excessively busy world we live in today, giving someone a small amount of your time can be a huge blessing. Whenever you help someone, you perform a blessing. This is a powerful thing to do as you're using your heart and mind in addition to divine energy to bless whoever or whatever it happens to be. As well as blessing other people, you can bless your home, your car, the weather, a plant or tree in your garden, and almost anything else. You shouldn't forget to bless yourself, either. In fact, you should bless yourself first before blessing others. You probably won't use your pendulum to bless others when you're out and about, but you can use it to enhance your blessings when doing them at home.

### • • • Exercise 17 • • •
### *How to Bless Others with Your Pendulum*

You can perform a blessing anywhere at any time. If you're walking along a street and decide to bless someone you happen to see, all you need do is silently say, "Bless you." If you're about to walk into a meeting, you can silently say a blessing to everyone attending. You'll find that your blessing will subtly change the way in which you interact with all the participants, and how they relate to you.

If you're performing blessings at home on your own, you can enhance them with the help of your pendulum.

1. Think of the person or object you're going to bless. If you know the person you're planning to bless, spend a minute or two remembering some of the happy times the two of you have shared. If you don't know the person, spend a moment or two

thanking the Divine for enabling you to make a blessing.

2. Take a deep breath and deliberately swirl your pendulum in a clockwise (positive) direction as you exhale.
3. Watch the pendulum as you silently send a blessing to the person or object you've been thinking about. Hold thoughts of love in your heart and mind until the pendulum stops rotating.
4. Close your eyes and feel a sense of peace for a moment before carrying on with your day or possibly making another blessing.

Most of us spend forty or more hours a week working at whatever we do to make a living. Your pendulum can help you make those hours more enjoyable and even suggest suitable careers if you're seeking a change or are looking for a new position. This important topic is the subject of the next chapter.

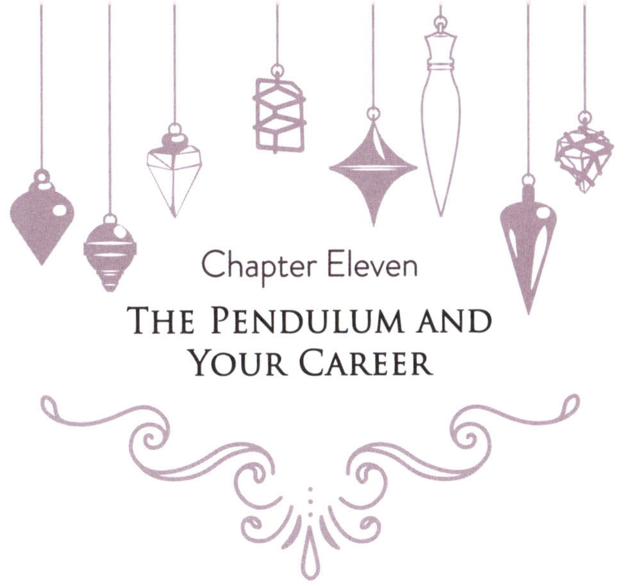

# Chapter Eleven
# The Pendulum and Your Career

Your pendulum is a powerful tool that can guide and help you in many areas of your life. Suppose you're reasonably happy in your work but feel as if you're in a rut and thinking about looking for a new position in another company. Before doing anything else, ask your pendulum if changing careers at this time would be beneficial to you in the long term. The answer to this is important. If you're ambitious, you're probably seeking a more senior role. You might want a position that is more intellectually satisfying than your current job. You could be thinking about making a change because of the time it takes to do your daily commute or because you want a position with more flexible hours to fit in with your family's needs. There could be many reasons why you think it's time for a change. While asking your pendulum questions, definitely ask if a career move would be positive for your home and family life.

Let's assume your pendulum's responses confirmed it was time to look for a new position and you start looking for suitable opportunities. Suddenly you hear of two positions that you think you'd enjoy doing. Should you apply for both in the hope of being offered one of them? Your pendulum could answer that but, before asking, ask it many questions about both opportunities. Start by asking your pendulum a series of questions about one of the two positions and make a note of your pendulum's responses. Then ask the same questions about the other opportunity.

You can ask any questions you wish, and they might include: Would I enjoy working for XYZ Company? Would I enjoy it more than my current job? Is the position likely to be too stressful for me? Will the job be challenging enough? Will I get along well with my new colleagues? Will I be able to handle the commute? Would the new position involve working longer hours? Is this company an ethical business?

By the time you've done this, you may have excluded one, or even both, of the positions. If both opportunities still interest you, you can ask your pendulum, "Would I be happier working at XYZ Company than I would at ABC Corporation?" If you're still unsure, you could reverse the companies and ask if you'd be happier working at ABC Corporation than you would at XYZ Company. Doing this can save you valuable time; you won't pursue positions that you wouldn't like or aren't suitable for your particular skills and interests.

You can also use your pendulum when you apply for the position. You can ask it if your résumé and cover letter need to be improved to attract attention. If you are asked for an in-person interview, you can ask your pendulum questions about the meeting itself, the person who'll be interviewing you, and the expected dress code.

Your pendulum can provide you with advice at every stage of your working life. It can help you choose a career that will be fulfilling and make the most of your talents and skills. It can help you assess job opportunities, avoid possible pitfalls, and provide advice on changing employers and even occupation.

# Questions to Ask When Choosing or Changing Your Career

- Would (specific career) provide me with fulfillment and happiness?
- Is this the right time to make an important career change?
- Will this career change benefit me in the long run?
- Will this career change provide a positive work-life balance?
- Will I be able to use my natural talents in this new opportunity?
- Does this career change provide opportunities to progress further in the future?
- Will this career change improve my financial position?
- Am I fully considering all other factors before making this change?
- Do I need to develop additional skills before making a change?

Someone entering the workforce for the first time is likely to ask the pendulum different questions to those asked by someone in mid-career. Someone seeking a part-time job will have different questions again. However, they'll all have some questions in common.

Before looking for a specific job, you'll find it helpful to make a list of all the things you've ever thought of doing for work. Include everything you have a talent or an aptitude for, total fantasies (such as an astronaut, movie star, president, or professional athlete), and any work you've done in the past. If other people have told you that you'd be good at something, include it in the list.

Once you've done this, hold your pendulum over each item on your list, one at a time, and ask the pendulum, "Would this be a good career for me?" Don't question your pendulum's response. Simply cross out the potential careers that your pendulum responded negatively to and move on to the next item on your list. By the time you're done, you'll have a number of possibilities to think about.

Wait at least twenty-four hours. The next day, write down the remaining items on your list on a different sheet of paper. Hold your pendulum over each item in turn and ask the same question, "Would this be a good career for me?" You may cross out a few more possibilities when you do this. Repeat this a day or two later and continue doing it until you have just one or two left. These will be the best careers to investigate further.

If you have two or three careers to think about, you can ask your pendulum further questions. You might ask, "Would I be happier working in (this career) than I would in (another career)?" "Would I progress more quickly in (this career) than I would in (another career)?" You can ask further questions about which career would be the most lucrative, personally satisfying, least stressful, and anything else you want to know. You can ask your pendulum the same questions about self-employment.

Now that you've worked out what career you are best suited for, you can start searching for work opportunities in that field. Everyone is different. Some people want work that pays well, while others are obviously interested in the pay but are more concerned about job satisfaction and future possibilitics. Make a list of your priorities and ask your pendulum how many of them would be met if you applied for a position at a particular company. Obviously your pendulum can't find work *for* you but will provide you with valuable information about any position you're thinking of applying for.

The next chapter teaches you how to use your pendulum to explore your past lives and find out what sort of person you were and what you did in previous lifetimes. It can also help you to look ahead and create your own future.

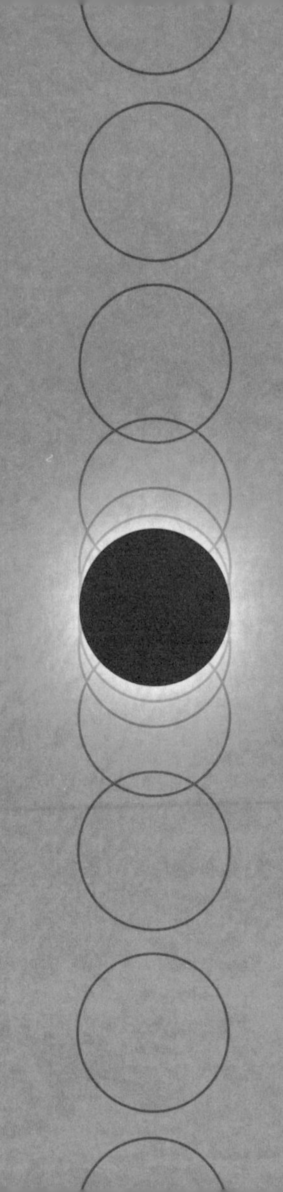

# Chapter Twelve
# Dowsing Your Past Lives

Have you ever wondered what sort of person you were in a past life? Your pendulum can tell you that and much more about the lives you had before this one. It can also give you information about historical figures, events, and places. People who use pendulums to research historic sites are called psychic archaeologists. Your pendulum can be helpful when practicing any form of divination, such as tarot, numerology, and astrology. You can also use your pendulum to ask questions about your future.

## How to Explore Your Past Lives

There are many ways to explore your past lives. Hypnotic regressions are the most popular because people who have them sense or "see" in their mind's eye different experiences they had in previous lives. Using a pendulum to explore your past lives is a much slower process but can produce a large amount of detailed information. People who've had hypnotic regressions often don't learn their dates of birth and death or find out where in the world they lived. Details of this sort are easy to determine using a pendulum.

### • • • Exercise 18 • • •
### *How to Learn About Your Past Lives*

Set aside at least thirty minutes of uninterrupted time. You'll need pen and paper to record your findings.

1. Finding out when you were born in your most recent past life or a particular lifetime you're exploring is your first step. Hold your pendulum and ask if you were born in the twentieth century in your last past life. Continue going back in time, century by century, until your pendulum gives a positive

response. Once you know the century ask if you were born in the first half of that century. If the answer is negative, you know you were born in the second half of that century. Ask your pendulum to confirm it to check that you're doing everything correctly. You can now ask your pendulum about different decades and then individual years until you've found your year of birth. If you wish, you can ask further questions to learn your month and day of birth. I usually stop after finding the year and come back to learn about specific dates only if I need them.

2. Next is finding out where you lived in this past lifetime. If you have a feeling that you lived in a particular place, ask your pendulum to confirm or deny this. Most of the time, you'll have to work your way through the alphabet, asking your pendulum if the first letter of the country you were born in was "A," "B," and so on until you get a positive response. Once you've found the first letter, you can ask about the second and other letters until you've learned the name

of the country. Once you have the name of the country, check this finding by asking your pendulum to confirm that you were born there. This is valuable information that is not possible to obtain in most other methods. In a past life regression, people often don't know what country they lived in, as in that lifetime they seldom traveled more than a few miles from the village or town they were born in.

3. Now that you know when and where you were born, you can ask about your sex. Ask your pendulum for confirmation as well.
4. The next step is to learn the name you had in that lifetime. Use the same process when finding out the name of the country you were born in, going through the alphabet again, one letter at a time. You can save time if the first few letters give you a clue as to what the name might be. If the pendulum spells out C-A-T, you could ask if your name was Catherine. If you're wrong, you can continue asking about individual letters until

you've spelled out the name. Once you have the name, confirm that it's correct by asking your pendulum, "Was my name (whatever it was) in this past life?"

5. You can now ask questions that reveal your occupation or the main way in which you spent your time. You can go through the alphabet again to do this. However, I prefer to start by asking about occupations that were likely to be common in the time and place of that past life. Examples are agriculture, fishing, teaching, healing, and child-rearing. If I don't get a positive response to one of those, I'll go through the alphabet again.
6. I find the results of this step fascinating. It's common for groups of people, especially close relatives and good friends, to be reincarnated together. Relationships and genders change, but the souls of the special people in this lifetime may well have been with you in previous lifetimes. Your sister in this lifetime might have been your father or daughter in the lifetime you're

exploring. Changes in sex are common and are necessary for us to experience every aspect of life. When doing this, I start by asking about my parents, wife, and children. I then continue by asking about other close relatives and good friends.

7. The next step is to learn more about your family in this lifetime. Start by asking if you were married and how many children you had. You can learn their sex, health, names, and anything else you want to know. In practice, I ask most of these questions later, as I find it more helpful to obtain a broad overview of my past life initially and return later to learn more details of any area that particularly interests me.
8. This is a good time to learn more about yourself. Were you outgoing and gregarious, or maybe quiet and shy? Were you studious and keen to learn? Did you go to school? Could you read and write? Did you have a wide circle of friends? Were you loved by others? Did you ever have time for hobbies

and other interests? Was it a happy lifetime? What talents did you have? Were you rich? Famous? Did you have a long or short life? Were you lonely in your old age? Once you get answers to some of these, you can ask further questions to gain more information and gradually build a picture of the person you were.

9. Now it's time to learn when you died. Rather than trying to determine the year of death, start by asking, "Was I over the age of fifty when I died?" You can then move forward in decades until you receive a negative response. Starting from the first previous positive response, go forward one year at a time until you find the exact age. Of course, if the pendulum said you were younger than fifty, you'd do the same process in reverse by going back one decade at a time. And as you can with your birth date, you can find the month and day of your death if you wish. In practice, I do this only if I intend to use the information

for genealogical research. You can also ask questions about how you died, who was present at your funeral, and anything else you'd like to know.

10. The final step is to find out what karma you built up during that lifetime that is having an effect on you in this lifetime. Start by asking if you have any karmic debts from this previous lifetime. Find out what areas of your life they're in. It's possible that you already know, but it's helpful to have it confirmed and discover other karmic factors you weren't already aware of. Ask your pendulum if you can repay the debt in this lifetime. Continue asking questions about it until you discover what you can do. Once you know what they are, you can start working on them, and your pendulum will keep you informed on how well you're progressing at repaying it.

. . . ( . . .

It can be a lengthy process to gain all the information you want. Fortunately, it's a pleasant task as you're gradually learning about one of your previous lifetimes. It's better to do one or two steps at each session rather than try to do it all in one marathon session.

You can explore as many of your past lives as you wish in the same way and also examine the past lives of family members and friends as long as you have their consent.

## Psychometry with Your Pendulum

Psychometry is the ability to sense vibrations from objects by touching or holding them. The most popular explanation of this phenomenon is that the object's history is preserved in its etheric body and can be felt by people who have trained themselves to sense the feelings and vibrations.

It's possible to pick up these feelings with your pendulum. All you need to do is to relax and hold your pendulum over the object you wish to psychometrize. It's best to start with an old object connected to you in some way, such as a family heirloom. When you do this, your pendulum may start showing its positive movement. It may give a completely different movement or even not move at all. What it does isn't important—the purpose of the exercise is to experience thoughts and feelings about the object. If the object belonged to a deceased relative, for example, you might suddenly feel close to that person or "hear" them talking to you, possibly giving you encouragement or expressing love. You may "taste" a favorite food that your relative made, "smell" a scent the person wore, or even "see" a scene from the person's life. If you repeat this exercise a day or two later, you'll learn more about the person and their life.

Once you've successfully psychometrized a number of objects with your pendulum, you can practice with objects you know nothing about and see what you can learn from them.

You may find that this is not the right time for you to become a psychometrist. If that's the case, you won't gain any feelings or sensations from objects you try to psychometrize but will have a feeling that this is not a good time for you to pursue psychometry. If this happens, forget about pendulum psychometry for a week or two before trying again.

# How Your Psychic Abilities Can Help Your Pendulum Work

Everyone has intuitive capabilities, and we all have hunches and feelings that can be used while working with the pendulum. Here are some of the more useful psychic abilities that you can use, often called the four "clairs."

**Clairaudience** is the ability to hear sounds and voices inside your head. These messages feel noticeably different from our usual inner narrator.

**Claircognizance** is the ability to know that something is about to occur or has already happened without using our usual faculties.

**Clairsentience** is the ability to sense emotions and energies psychically. A common example is to meet someone for the first time and to instantly like or dislike them for no apparent reason.

**Clairvoyance** is the ability to become aware of mental images or visions without using the normal senses. It's a sense of knowing about something.

## How to Clarify and Enhance Your Psychic Readings with Your Pendulum

Your pendulum can play a useful role in any form of divination. It can, for instance, determine which questions are the best ones to ask before you start the reading. I do this by writing all the questions I can think of on pieces of paper and then hold my pendulum over each one in turn while asking, "Is this the most useful question I can ask today?" Sometimes your pendulum may not respond positively over any of the cards when you ask this question. If this happens, you have the opportunity to ask, "Is there a better, more insightful question that I could ask?" If you get a yes response to this, you need to ask further questions to determine what to ask. It's likely to be because you've asked questions about love, for example, when the most helpful reading for your client at this time might be work and finance.

Your pendulum can choose the cards to read when you're doing a tarot, angel, or oracle card reading. After mixing the cards, spread them face down across a table and ask your pendulum to indicate the cards selected for the reading. If you have a number of decks, your pendulum can tell you which one would be the best to use today. Your pendulum can also confirm or deny anything you say during a reading as well. If you do the reading while holding your pendulum, it will react positively or negatively to everything you say.

If you're uncertain about what a particular spread means, you can ask your pendulum questions about it to make sure that you give the correct answer. You can also hold your pendulum over each card in turn and ask as many questions as necessary to clarify the situation. At the end of a reading, you can ask your pendulum if you have covered everything that your client needs to know.

Your pendulum can also be useful whenever you're looking for a new deck. While holding it over any potential deck that appeals to you, ask it if this is the right deck for you to purchase today.

## Looking Into the Future

Your thoughts and actions today create your future. People who are lazy today will still be lazy twenty years from now unless they change their outlook and their lives. Many people drift through life, living from day to day without making any long-term plans or goals. They're like ships without rudders. Fortunately with the help of your pendulum, you can take control and create the future you want.

### • • • Exercise 19 • • •

### *How to Create the Future You Desire*

1. This first step is done without your pendulum. Set aside about thirty minutes of quiet time on your own. I prefer to do this in the evening when it's dark. Make sure the room is warm enough. Sit down in a comfortable chair, close your eyes, relax, and let your mind drift. Think about the life you're leading now, and then let your mind move forward about a year. What would you like your life to be like twelve months from now? What do you need to do to make this ideal life a reality? Would your life be better if you made those changes? Are you prepared to pay the price? Continue thinking about your life twelve months from now until you feel you've seen enough. Mentally move forward and visualize the life you'd like to be living five years from now. Are your important relationships going well? Are you noticeably better off financially than you were five years ago? Is your health better or worse? How is your spiritual life? Think

about what you need to do to achieve this ideal life and ask yourself if you're prepared to do whatever needs to be done to achieve it. Five years is probably far enough in the future to start with. However, there's no limit. If you wish, you can project yourself ten, twenty, or any other number of years into the future.

2. Once you've done this, take a few slow, deep breaths and open your eyes. Think about what your life will be like twelve months (and five years) from now. Write down as much as you can remember about your life at these times. The chances are you'll be happy with your potential future life but may have doubts about your ability to achieve them.
3. Wait a day or two before moving on to the second step. While you're waiting, you'll spend some time thinking about your future and may even start making plans on how to change what's preventing you from moving ahead.

4. When you're ready, sit down again with pen and paper and think about what you learned in the visualization about what your life will be like twelve months from now. Write down everything you want to change. If you want to earn more money than the visualization indicated, decide how much money you want to earn and then make a list of everything you can think of that you could do to improve your financial situation. It doesn't matter how unlikely some of the ideas may be—your pendulum will help you decide which ones to pursue later.
5. Repeat this with everything you want to change. Everyone wants more money, but you might also want to improve your relationships, continue with your education, start a physical fitness program, become a better partner and parent, and learn how to play a musical instrument. Make a list of everything you can think of that would help you achieve these goals. One effective way to make this as comprehensive as possible

is to write the obituary you would wish to have read at your funeral. As no one will see this you can include everything you hope to achieve in this lifetime, such as your business successes, your skills and talents, and the service you gave to the community. You should also include your creative and artistic interests, your home and family life, and your interest in health and outdoor activities. Add everything you haven't yet accomplished to your lists.

6. The next step is to hold your pendulum over each item on your lists and ask it the following questions about each one:
    - Is this idea realistic?
    - Will this idea help me lead the life I want to be living twelve months (or five years) from now?
    - Will I remain motivated enough to achieve it?
    - Is this goal too ambitious for me?

- Is the price I'll need to pay to achieve this goal in terms of time and effort too high?
- You can ask your pendulum further questions to clarify anything you're not sure about. Your pendulum will tell you what items on your lists to discard, and which ones to pursue.

7. With the help of your pendulum, rewrite the items you're going to work on in order of importance, and then create a plan of action to make your dream a reality.

I've met many people who reached the last stage but then failed to act to make it happen. If you experience this, repeat the exercises in chapter 9—the problem could be motivation, confidence, and doubts about your ability to make it happen. Once you've done that, visualize the life you want to be leading one year from now again. Then pick up your pendulum, close your eyes, and say, "This is the life I want. I'm prepared to pay the price." When you open your eyes, your pendulum should be giving your positive response. If it isn't, you can repeat the exercise again, or, alternatively, ask your pendulum to help you find out why your subconscious mind is holding you back.

. . . ( . . .

In the next chapter we're going to take a large step forward and use our pendulums to develop and grow spiritually. In the process, we'll also cover psychic protection and manifestation.

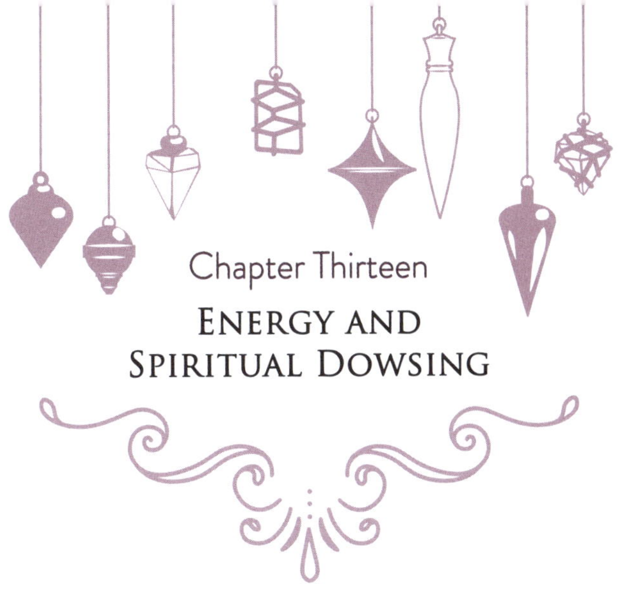

# Chapter Thirteen
# Energy and Spiritual Dowsing

Almost everything we've done so far includes information that our pendulums obtained from our higher selves. It should be no surprise that your pendulum can help you go well beyond this and gain information from the subtle realms. Everything in the universe expresses energies with the ability to affect the physical, emotional, and spiritual aspects of your being. Consequently, your pendulum can be used to develop your intuition and for spiritual explorations, including connecting with angels, spirit guides, and even your own soul.

## Dowsing Your Spirit Guides

Spirit guides are people who have lived on earth but are currently in between lives. They have reached a high spiritual level but retain an interest in what is happening in this world. Some spirit guides are souls who do not need to reincarnate again. Spirit guides are willing to help, guide, and support us whenever we ask them for advice. Because they've learned the lessons we're trying to master, they act as mentors and advisors. However, they are primarily concerned with your spiritual growth and do not appreciate being asked for help whenever a problem arises that you could easily resolve yourself.

Spirit guides are assigned to you at birth; some say we all have a specific number of guides to watch over and guide us through life. The usual number is seven. However, my belief is that everyone has as many guides as they need; as people grow and develop, they often need different guides from the ones they started life with.

Many people go through life without ever communicating with their spirit guides. This is because spirit guides don't offer advice unless someone asks for it. However, if one of these people was in a desperate situation and called on God (or whatever name they call the Divine) for help, aid would come immediately from that person's spirit guides. Events that are put down to coincidences are sometimes examples of help from spirit guides.

Spirit guides are frequently deceased relatives who continue to provide help and guidance from the other side. It's comforting to know that someone who was important to us in the past is still providing comfort and support whenever you need it.

There are many ways to communicate with your spirit guides, such as the Ouija board, automatic writing, mediums, telepathy, intuition, and dreams. Sometimes messages from your guides are delivered through friends and strangers who are usually unaware that they are passing a message on to you. The pendulum has been used to communicate with spirit guides since the early days of the Spiritualist movement (the mid-nineteenth century) and is a highly effective way to communicate with them.

As always, the most important part of the process is your intent. There's not much point in contacting your guides simply to say hello. However, if your intent is strong and you want to speak to a guide for help in a particular matter, to contact a deceased relative, or simply to ask for support and encouragement, you'll make a connection quickly and easily.

Sit down in a peaceful place where you're unlikely to be interrupted. Place your pendulum next to you. Close your eyes and take several slow, deep breaths. As you do, think about your intent.

Open your eyes and pick up your pendulum. Silently or out loud, say, "Spirit guides, I'm ready and waiting to communicate with you. Is this a good time to talk?" Sit quietly and wait for a response. As you're holding your pendulum, it will probably give a positive response. However, you may experience a sense of warmth, feel a gentle touch, or some other sensation instead. Be alert to any response. Many times, I thought I'd failed to make contact but realized later that I did receive a response but failed to notice it. Your pendulum will usually respond positively because your guides are always keen to make contact. However, as there will be times that are inconvenient to them, there's no need to feel let down or rejected if you receive a negative response. When that happens, try again in an hour or two.

As soon as you experience any form of contact, say thank you. You've now established contact on both sides and can start asking any questions you wish. You may receive a response immediately, usually through the pendulum. Always respond with a "thank you" every time you receive a message. Some of your questions may not be answered immediately, and you may have to wait a few days for the answer. When this happens, ask the question again every day until you receive an answer.

Even if you have no specific questions, you can learn more about the spirit guide you are communicating with. You can ask for your guide's name, for instance. With questions like this, the answer will usually come as a thought in your mind.

With practice, you'll be able to communicate with your spirit guides virtually immediately, most of the time. On rare occasions, you might have to try again an hour or two later. As you do this, you'll learn more and more about the spirit world and the guides who are there to help you.

## Dowsing Your Angels

Angels are supernatural beings of thought who mediate between the Divine and humankind. The word "angel" comes from the Greek word *angelos*, which means "messenger." Many people are unaware that they were assigned a guardian angel either at the moment of conception or the time of birth, who has the task of protecting, guiding, and looking after you throughout this lifetime. In the Christian tradition, your guardian angel carries your soul up to heaven when you die. It's possible that your guardian angel stays with you throughout all your incarnations and consequently knows more about you than anyone else. This angel looks after your soul as well as your physical body.

Most of the time, your guardian angel will offer advice only when it's asked for. Everyone makes mistakes at times, and it's reasonable to wonder why our guardian angels don't step in and prevent them from happening. The reason is that we learn from our mistakes; oftentimes they teach us the lessons we need to learn in this lifetime.

Guardian angels communicate with their charges through dreams, thoughts, and intuitions. As they speak to us with a "still small voice" (I Kings 19:12), what they tell us can be easily overlooked. You need to pay attention to their messages, which appear as thoughts in our minds.

Fortunately with the help of your pendulum, you can communicate with your guardian angel and any other angel whenever you wish. I know people who communicate with their guardian angel solely through the pendulum. Others use their pendulum to ask if their guardian angel is ready to talk with them and then lay their pendulums down and continue the conversation by speaking silently or out loud to their angel. Their angels respond by placing messages in their mind. I know many people who started contacting their guardian angel with a pendulum but no longer need it to communicate after establishing a connection. I usually talk directly with my guardian angel, though sometimes I still use my pendulum. The manner in which I communicate depends on my needs at the time.

If you wish, you can include the angels every time you use your pendulum by asking: "Do I have the angels' blessing to ask the questions I'm going to ask?" A positive response lets you know that the angels are present and will give you whatever help and support you may need. If you get a negative response, you'll need to ask further questions to find out why they're not willing to bless your session with the pendulum. A common reason for a negative response is that you've (hopefully inadvertently) overlooked the needs of other people who are involved with the questions you're going to ask. It's also possible that the angels think you're perfectly capable of working out the answer without needing a pendulum. This happens when people become overly reliant on their pendulums and start using them for every decision they make. Occasionally, I see people dowsing fruit and vegetables to determine which ones they'll buy. This is a good idea if they're checking them for chemicals or tampering, but a pendulum isn't necessary to decide whether to buy them—this kind of decision can be made just as well without one.

I almost always have a pendulum with me; I wear it around my neck. It acts as an amulet and lucky charm as well as a dowsing device. However, I use it only when I can't determine an answer on my own. Consequently, I may not use it for a few weeks and then dowse with it several times in one week. I don't hesitate to use it when I feel it's necessary but don't want it to become a crutch, either.

## How to Ask Your Guardian Angel Multi-Choice Questions

Your guardian angel is willing to help you decide the right choice from a number of possibilities. You can do this for anything you wish such as the best vacation destination, the best location to move to, the right house to buy, the most suitable job or career, and anything else that involves a choice.

You can do this by asking your guardian angel about each possibility individually by holding your pendulum over whatever it happens to be. If the object is too large or isn't with you, you can use a photograph or write the name and other details on a piece of paper. This can be time-consuming, especially if you have a large selection of items to consider.

It's much easier to write all the possibilities on different cards or pieces of paper and ask your guardian angel to make your pendulum give a positive response when held over the item that will be best for you.

A good friend of mine collects porcelain chickens on baskets and spends a great deal of time searching for them online and in antique stores. Unfortunately, she can't afford to buy every chicken she finds. If she has a number to choose from, she'll write down the details of each one on separate pieces of paper and ask her guardian angel to select the right one for her to purchase. She's happy with the decisions her guardian angel makes, and it's saved her time and money. I also know someone who bought a used car using the same method. He asked his guardian angel to indicate which car would be most reliable, economical to run, and within his budget. He is extremely happy with his purchase.

## Close a Session with a Spirit, Angel, or Guide

Your pendulum plays a valuable role in bringing a ritual or session to a close. Start by thanking the spirit, angel, or spirit guide (by name if possible) for being there during the ritual and ensuring its success. Suspend your pendulum; if it swings in clockwise circles, it's a sign that your gratitude has been received. If it fails to move or gives a different response, take a slow and deep breath, and repeat your words of gratitude. Ask if the presence has received your thanks.

Next, release the guide. Say something similar to: "It's now time for me to release you. Please go in peace. Thank you for everything you've done." Again, suspend your pendulum. If it doesn't move in clockwise circles, ask: "Has (name) left in peace?"

To finish, hold your pendulum and say: "The ritual is now complete. Thank you. Thank you. Thank you." When it stops moving, move a short distance away from the area of the ritual and ground yourself by having something to eat and drink.

## How to Communicate with Deceased Relatives and Loved Ones

As well as communicating with spirit guides and angels with the help of your pendulum, you can also use it to communicate with deceased relatives and other loved ones. As this is usually a comforting and spiritual conversation, you need to set aside at least thirty minutes (preferably longer) in a quiet place where you're unlikely to be interrupted.

Rather than leave the conversation entirely up to whatever thoughts occur to you in the moment, it's more helpful to write a list of questions that you're seeking answers to. Until I started writing my questions beforehand, I'd often later think of questions that I should have asked during the session. I also like to begin with simple questions and move on to more specific questions once they've been answered.

Ground yourself and then spend a minute or two thinking about the person you want to communicate with. When you feel relaxed and ready to start, hold your pendulum and say your intention. For instance, you might say, "I'd like to have a conversation with (deceased person) today and I seek his/her guidance on what is going on in my life. It would be comfortable and healing for me. I ask to be surrounded with positivity and love throughout our conversation."

Pause until your pendulum gives your positive response and then ask if your deceased relative is with you. After this second positive response, you can ask questions about anything you wish to know. You might ask if the person is happy and at peace. You could ask if there's anything you can do for him or her in your world. You should certainly ask if the person has any messages or advice for you and talk for as long as you wish. Finish by thanking the person for their guidance, support, and love.

The answers will come through the pendulum's responses as well as your intuition. Don't be disappointed if your first experiments are not as exciting or revealing as you'd hoped. It's important to be patient, kind, and loving to recognize and interpret the often-subtle messages. It takes time to master spirit communication.

Don't try to force answers if the person you're communicating with is not forthcoming; there'll be a reason, and you may decide to let the question go or ask it again later. As you communicate with your chosen person, you may become overcome with emotions. If this happens, it's best to close the session down and try again at a later date.

## Psychic Protection with Your Pendulum

Psychic protection involves protecting your aura from negative energies. This forms an invisible cocoon that surrounds us and protects us from psychic attack. Everyone needs psychic protection at times; we all suffer from stresses, pressures, and other forms of negativity on a regular basis as we go through life. Even our own negative thoughts pull us down and can be considered as self-inflicted psychic attacks.

People have used different methods of psychic protection for thousands of years. Amulets and lucky charms have been found in prehistoric cave dwellings. These were probably worn to provide protection. People still wear amulets and charms today and also use crystals, gemstones, scents, prayers, and rituals to help keep them safe.

The quickest way to provide psychic protection to a house, person, animal, or plant is to say a prayer while swinging your pendulum in a clockwise rotation. While the pendulum is moving ask the Divine to remove any negativity, enhance the positivity, and protect whatever it happens to be. Complete the ritual by performing a blessing.

Chapter 2 covered how to protect yourself while using your pendulum. You can also use your pendulum to provide protection in other situations as well.

## How to Protect Your Home and Workplace

You can protect your home, workplace, and anywhere else where you spend time by asking your pendulum to rid it of all negativity. Most are energies formed as a result of frustrations, arguments, tensions, and stress. They usually dissolve and disappear quickly, but ongoing problems in a room can create negative thought-forms that refuse to dissipate and make the space feel uncomfortable.

### • • • Exercise 20 • • •

### *How to Clear Negative Energies in a House*

There are two versions of this exercise: The first contains everything necessary to eliminate negative energies in a house that is known to have them, and the second can be used to clear a house that may or may not contain any negativity.

#### Version One

1. Start by opening all the windows in the house. After doing so, stand at the main entrance and ask your pendulum if there

is anything inside the building detrimental to the well-being of everyone living there. As you already know or at least suspect, that the house contains negative energies, your pendulum will probably give a positive response.

2. Ask your pendulum to lead you to the room that contains the most negative energies and circle when you reach the door to that room.
3. While standing at the entrance to the room, ask your pendulum to indicate the direction of the negativity and circle when you reach the exact location.
4. Stop the movements of your pendulum once it starts circling. Talk to the negative energy in your normal speaking voice. Some dowsers like to turn a house clearing into a theatrical event but that's not what the clearing is about. You might say: "I know you're trapped and need help and healing. I'm going to swing my pendulum counterclockwise, and this will remove you from this space and take you into the

light where you will receive all the love and healing you need." Pause for a few moments before swinging your pendulum. Stand quietly until it stops moving. Say, "Thank you. I'm now going to swing my pendulum clockwise. This will fill this room with positive energy, providing joy, peace, and love to everyone who uses it."

5. Stand quietly until the pendulum stops moving. Ask it: "Is this room completely cleared of all negativities?" If your pendulum says no, ask it to guide you to the area of negativity and repeat steps four and five. If your pendulum gives a positive response, ask it if there are any other rooms in the house that contain negativity. If there are, perform steps 2 to 5 again to eliminate the problems.
6. Once your pendulum has removed all the negativity in the affected rooms, stand in the center of all the other rooms in turn, swing your pendulum in a clockwise direction, and say: "I'm filling this room with positive energy. At the same time, any lingering

adverse energies will dissipate and go to the light. This room is being filled with joy, love, and vibrant energy."

7. After you've filled each room with positive energy, return to the main entrance and ask your pendulum: "Is there anything inside this house detrimental to the well-being of the people who live here?" Your pendulum should now give a negative response. Thank your pendulum for helping you free the home of all negative energy.
8. Use your pendulum to send a blessing to the house and everyone who lives in it. Wait at least five minutes before closing any windows.

It happens infrequently, but there's a slight possibility that your pendulum will give a positive response to the last question. This is because some thought-forms can be difficult to clear, especially if the factors that caused them in the first place are still present in the house. If this happens, ask your pendulum to indicate the area that is still causing problems and repeat steps 3 to 5.

### Version Two

1. Open all the windows in the house. Stand at the main entrance to the house and ask your pendulum if there is anything inside the building that is detrimental to the well-being of everyone living there. If you get a positive response to this question, perform version one of this exercise. If you get a negative response, swirl your pendulum clockwise and send a blessing to the house and everyone who lives in it.
2. Stand in the center of each room in the house in turn and ask if there are any negative energies in the room. You should receive a negative response. When this occurs, spin the pendulum in a clockwise direction and fill the room with positive energy. It's unlikely you'll receive a positive response in any of the rooms, but if you do, ask your pendulum to indicate where in the room the negative energy is. Tell the negative energy: "I know you're trapped and need help and healing. I'm going to swing

my pendulum counterclockwise to send you into the light where you will receive the love and healing you need." Pause for a few moments before swinging your pendulum. Stand quietly until it stops moving. Say, "Thank you. I'm now going to swing my pendulum clockwise. This will fill this room with positive energy, providing joy, peace, and love to everyone who uses it."

3. Once you've filled all the rooms with positive energy, spin your pendulum in a clockwise direction and walk through the house, making sure to enter every room. When you reach the front door, pause and wait until your pendulum stops moving. Finish by using your pendulum to send a blessing to the house and everyone who lives in it. Wait for at least five minutes before closing any windows.

In recent years, many books have been written about manifesting whatever it is you want using the law of attraction. Your pendulum can enhance every stage of the process, from deciding what to manifest to achieving it. The essential five steps to successful manifestation are the subject of the next chapter.

Chapter Fourteen

# Manifestation with Your Pendulum

The word "manifestation" originally referred to something spiritual that could become a reality, for example an idea becoming real in a person's life. In recent years, the word has become associated with attracting wealth and abundance, though it is much broader than that. Manifestation occurs when someone focuses on their goals and aspirations, believes they can achieve them, and then makes them a reality. It's possible to manifest a promotion at work, a life partner, or anything else, by deciding on the goal, believing it is possible, and attracting it to you.

Your pendulum can help you manifest anything you want. In this instance, it's being used as a magical tool rather than a dowsing instrument. We've already deliberately made our pendulums spin in clockwise and counterclockwise directions. Counterclockwise, spinning to the left, is used to eliminate something, such as ill health. Spinning your pendulum clockwise attracts whatever it is you want, which may include vibrant health or bucket-loads of money.

The law of attraction says that we attract whatever it is we focus on. However, it won't work if you decide you want to attract a million dollars and then do nothing to make it happen. You need to believe that your goal is possible and be prepared to do whatever is necessary to make it happen, which will take time and effort. Most people fail to achieve their manifestation goals because they don't stay focused on what they want and give up as soon as the road ahead looks too difficult. Many people are also distracted by other hopes, dreams, and fantasies that divert them from their main goal. Your pendulum can keep you on track with all of these.

If you have a good positive attitude, believe you can achieve your goal, and are prepared to do whatever hard work is necessary to make it happen, your pendulum will give you additional motivation and energy to help make your goal a reality. You already know that spinning your pendulum clockwise attracts what you want. Your pendulum will keep you on track when you use it in a ritual that attracts your goal to you. It will also keep you motivated, enable you to maintain a positive attitude, and enhance your belief—and that's real magic.

The first step is to decide exactly what it is you want to manifest (your intention). It needs to be as clear as possible. An intention to manifest a million dollars is not as useful as an intention to own a beautiful home. In this case, if you intend to use the million dollars to buy your dream home, it is better to make the home your intention, rather than a specific sum of money. However, you can go deeper than this. Why do you want a million-dollar home? In some places, a million dollars would buy a mansion, while it might buy only a small apartment somewhere else. Let's assume it will buy a really good home where you live. Do you want to own a million-dollar house to impress others? That's not an especially good intention. What would owning a million-dollar house do for you? It would provide a home for you and your family, of course. Would it enable you to stop paying rent and live in your own home? Would you be able to afford the ongoing costs of owning a million-dollar home? Would you be happier living in a million-dollar home than you would in a cheaper home? Ask your pendulum as many questions of this sort as you can to discover the underlying reasons for your particular intent.

Let's assume you want the million dollars because you intend to use it to help charities in your area. That's a worthy intent, but you're restricting yourself to a specific sum of money. Would you be able to help people in your area with less or greater amounts of money? Of course. In this case, a better intention might be to regularly receive money and other tangible items that could be used to help others. With the right questions, your pendulum could also uncover your motivations for this particular intention. Are you doing this for purely altruistic reasons? Would it make you feel important? Are you doing it to impress others?

As you can see, you need to spend time thinking about what you want to manifest and ask your pendulum questions at every stage.

The second step is belief. You must believe that you will manifest your intention. This is easier said than done as we all harbor self-limiting beliefs that hold us back and prevent us from achieving our goals. It's impossible to achieve our intentions as long as we hold negative beliefs about them. Fortunately, negative beliefs exist only as long as we decide they're true. Your pendulum will tell you what, if any, limiting beliefs you're holding about your intention.

Hold your pendulum and say your intention out loud. Your pendulum will respond, usually with a positive or negative movement. A positive response shows that your intention and belief are in harmony with each other. A negative response is a sign that you're holding negative beliefs about it. You may have a number of negative beliefs that need to be dealt with before you start working on your intention. For instance, you may feel unworthy and don't deserve to have the intention. You may have subconscious fears about what other people will think, or your ability to do the necessary work. If your intention involves money, you may be subconsciously limited by beliefs that you accepted when you were a child. "Money doesn't grow on trees" is a common example (see chapter 9).

There are two ways to deal with negative beliefs. You can deal with them individually by asking your pendulum questions about your limiting beliefs and removing them one at a time. Alternatively, you can spin your pendulum counterclockwise while telling yourself that you're eliminating every negative belief that relates to your intention. Keep focused on this until your pendulum comes to a stop. Spin your pendulum clockwise this time while telling yourself that you're filling your body, mind, and soul with positive, constructive beliefs that will help you achieve your intention. When the pendulum stops moving, say thank you to the universe for enabling you to become the person you want to be. Don't be in a hurry to see if this ritual has worked. Wait until the following day and then say your intention out loud while holding your pendulum.

As you've been holding on to these self-limiting beliefs for many years, maybe since you were a small child, you'll probably need to repeat this exercise several times until all of them have disappeared. You'll have made a big step forward when your pendulum gives you a positive response showing that your intention and beliefs are working for you.

The third step is to keep a positive mental attitude about your intention. I find it better to keep my manifestation goals secret, as friends and family either cast doubt on what I'm doing or expect it to magically happen in a short period of time. When I wake up in the morning, I think about my intention and briefly see myself as I'll be once it has been accomplished. In effect, I start the day feeling positive about my intention, a feeling that remains with me throughout the day. This feeling also keeps me motivated, and that motivation helps me feel willing to do whatever work is required to make the intention a reality. Every day I perform a ritual that includes all five essentials to manifesting desires: intention, belief, motivation, a positive attitude, and hard work.

## Manifestation Ritual

This ritual can be shortened or lengthened depending on how much time you have available. Even on days when you can't perform the ritual, spend a few minutes focusing on your intent while spinning your pendulum clockwise. Whenever possible, perform at least part of the ritual and do this every day until you've achieved success.

# How to Establish a Daily Manifestation Practice

To achieve your manifestation goals, you need to keep focused on whatever it is you are manifesting. A daily practice with your pendulum will help you do that.

1. Write out whatever it is you wish to manifest in large letters on a sheet of 8½ x 11 paper. You also need to compile a list of ten affirmations. You can change these whenever you wish.
2. Hold your pendulum, close your eyes, and visualize a stream of golden light descending from the infinite and filling you with positive energy. Open your eyes, look at your pendulum and say something along the lines of: "I align with my highest good and ask for guidance to manifest abundance for my loved ones and myself." Your pendulum should give you your positive response. If it does, you can move on with the ritual. If it doesn't, there is a blockage that needs to be eliminated before proceeding. Ask your

pendulum if you need to take a particular action before proceeding. If necessary, recite some affirmations and then ask again.

3. At this stage, ask your pendulum questions about your manifestation goal. You could ask if there's any specific action you could do today to move toward your goal. You might ask what positive emotions will help you today.
4. Hold your pendulum over your sheet of 8½ x 11 paper. Read what you wrote and the ask: "Would you strengthen and increase this energy for my highest good?" Wait to see if your pendulum gives a positive response.
5. Thank your pendulum for helping you and revolve it in a clockwise direction over your words. When it stops moving, thank it again and finish by saying, "I trust the universe and release any attachments I might have about my request."

### • • • Exercise 21 • • •
### *How to Manifest with Your Pendulum*

1. Find a quiet place to perform the ritual, and make sure you won't be interrupted for about thirty minutes. I use my sacred space because I enter into the right state of mind as soon as I walk into the room.
2. Place three candles on a table or altar in front of where you'll be working. I usually have white candles but use red candles if I need motivation and green candles when I need to put hard work and effort into any matters concerning my intention. Place your pendulum on your altar too.
3. Stand or sit in front of your altar, close your eyes, and visualize a pure white light descending from Divine Spirit that completely surrounds you with peace and protection. In your mind's eye, see the white light continuing to descend until it has surrounded you, your altar, and the room you're in.

4. Take three deep breaths using what is known as the physiological sigh, a double inhale followed by a lengthy exhale. You do this by inhaling through your nose until your lungs are almost full. Pause for a moment and then continue inhaling until your lungs are full. Exhale slowly through your mouth and continue exhaling until your lungs are completely empty. Breathing this way releases more carbon dioxide than normal breathing, reduces stress, and enables you to fully relax in a matter of seconds.
5. Open your eyes, light the candles, pick up your pendulum, and spin it in a clockwise direction. Think about your intention and why it is important to you. Allow a feeling of enthusiasm and excitement to reach every part of your body with the attitude that you know you'll achieve it. When you reach this state, tell yourself that you are attracting your intention to you and it is getting closer every day. Continue focusing on your thoughts and feelings about your intention until your pendulum stops moving.

6. Look at the flames of the candles and focus on your heart. Know with every fiber of your being that your intention will manifest. Feel a sense of enthusiasm and excitement in your heart as you silently affirm this.
7. Swing your pendulum clockwise again. This time, visualize yourself after having achieved your intent. See it as clearly as possible in your mind's eye and also include smell, taste, hearing, and touch in the picture. Feel how excited and happy you'll be once you've achieved this goal. See yourself celebrating with your family and close friends. Make everything as real as you can. Celebrate everything associated with your success. It's yours and you deserve it.
8. Hold on to these thoughts and feelings until your pendulum stops moving. Put your pendulum down and thank the Divine for enabling you to achieve your intention. Snuff out the candles, get up, and have something small to eat and drink. I usually

have a handful of nuts and raisins and a glass of water.

9. Carry on with your day, trusting that your intention is on its way.

As soon as possible after performing this ritual, do something that takes you a step closer to your goal. This could be reading or watching a YouTube video on a subject that relates to your intent. It might be talking with someone who is in a position to help you. It could be a physical action. No matter what it is, do it with joy in your heart, as you know it will help you achieve your goal.

## How to Manifest Love

Although many people associate manifestation with money, you can manifest anything you wish into your life, and most would find it hard to think of anything more important than manifesting a special person to love. Your pendulum can help you in all matters involving love and romance ranging from strengthening your current relationship to attracting the love you deserve.

There are a number of things you need to do before performing a manifestation ritual. Start by asking your pendulum if you're ready for a new relationship. Is there any baggage from the past that needs to be resolved before you commit yourself to a new relationship? Are you open to attracting love? Why do you want a new relationship? Should you start looking for a new relationship at this time? Are you holding on to any limiting beliefs that could prevent you from finding love?

If necessary, create positive affirmations to help you overcome your limiting beliefs. You can also write affirmations to attract the right person to you. Test each affirmation with your pendulum to make sure that it is right for you. Here are some examples:

- I am a lovable person who deserves love and happiness.
- I let go of all the negativity from my past.
- Love is safe for me.
- I attract love everywhere I go.
- I am open to giving and receiving love.
- I deserve a partner who loves and respects me.
- I trust the universe to bring the right partner to me.
- The right person is coming my way.

Assuming you've decided to seek a loving relationship, the next step is to decide what you want in a partner. Make a list of all the positive qualities you want this person to have. Obviously you want your partner to be kind, loving, and honest. You also need to specify interests that you want to share. If, for instance, you love travel, you'll want to list travel as an interest you'll share. Do you have any preferences as far as the person's age, ethnicity, height, occupation, and location? If so, include them in your list.

It's best to do this list over a few days to allow several ideas to come into your mind once you start thinking about your future partner. Write them all down.

Use this list to create some affirmations (see chapter 9) that include these qualities. Be as specific as possible. You may, for instance, have written down that you want your future partner to be interested in music, but that is far too broad. If you love orchestral chamber music, you're likely to have problems living with someone who wants to listen to heavy metal all the time.

Once you've completed the list, hold your pendulum over each quality in turn while thinking about your future partner. It should respond positively to each one. If your pendulum gives a negative response to any of the qualities you wrote down, ask further questions to find out why it responded that way. The problem might be in the way you worded the quality. It could relate to something painful that happened to you in the past. Whatever it is, ask further questions, and remove that quality from your list if necessary.

If you haven't already included it on your list, add: "I am worthy of true love." Because many people have had problems and difficulties in relationships in the past, they underrate themselves and settle for second-best. It's important to believe that you're worthy of the person of your dreams. Hold your pendulum, close your eyes, and say this affirmation out loud. Silently count to five, open your eyes, and see what your pendulum is saying.

If it's showing a positive response, you can start performing the love attraction ritual. If you receive a negative response, you'll have to work on your self-esteem until you receive a positive response (see chapter 9). Test the affirmation with your pendulum every day until you receive the response you need. Once you've done all of this, perform the love manifestation ritual every day or two until you've achieved your goal.

### • • • Exercise 22 • • •

## *How to Manifest Love with Your Pendulum*

As this ritual involves candles, make sure you have a container of water close by in case of accident.

1. Place and light some white, pink, and red candles on your altar. White candles relate to peace, serenity, and happiness, pink candles relate to love, tenderness, and harmony, and red candles relate to passion and excitement. As you light them, think of the qualities each of these colors will bring into your relationship.
2. Sit down approximately three feet away from the candles, swing your pendulum clockwise, and read (preferably out loud) the positive affirmations you've created about yourself and your feelings about love. Repeat the affirmations until your pendulum stops moving.
3. Put your pendulum down, close your eyes, smile, and visualize yourself as you are now that your mind has accepted all the positive

affirmations. Hold this visualization as long as you can. Open your eyes.

4. Swing your pendulum clockwise and read the list of positive qualities your future partner will share with you. Read the list over and over again until your pendulum stops moving.
5. Put your pendulum down, close your eyes, and think of the happy times you and your new partner will spend together in the future. Relate some of these thoughts to the interests you both will share, and also "see" your partner and you at different times in the future as you grow older together, still cherishing and loving each other.
6. When you feel ready, open your eyes and say a prayer of thanks to the Divine for bringing your partner to you. Snuff out the candles and ground yourself by eating and drinking something before returning to your everyday life.

# Conclusion

The pendulum is a wonderful tool that can be used for many purposes. I hope you've discovered some for yourself while trying out the different exercises in this book. You may not have succeeded at every one, but remember that it takes time and practice to become a skilled dowser. Congratulate yourself on your successes and also think about the experiments that didn't work as well as you'd hoped. It's possible that your mind strayed and you forgot to think of your intent. You could have been distracted by something else occurring near you. Your intent may not have been clear. You may have forgotten to ask, "Can I?", "May I?", and "Should I?" You may have been dehydrated or hungry. You could have been trying too hard. Grim determination doesn't always work—in fact, it frequently makes success impossible. Approach your pendulum work with serious intent but maintain your sense of humor and levity. Above all, have fun while doing it.

You now know that you can operate your pendulum in one part of the world and be able to make a difference to the life of someone living thousands of miles away from you, such as when you send love or forgiveness to someone. Distance makes no difference, and you'll find you'll be able to balance someone's chakras, for instance, using online video chat programs. Whenever possible, I like to be able to see the person I'm working with, but it's possible to dowse just as effectively over the phone or computer as in person.

As you develop your skills, you're bound to come across skeptical people who might laugh or scoff at your interest in the pendulum. You won't gain anything by trying to show them how the pendulum works as their negativity and preconceived ideas ensure that the pendulum won't work in their hands. In fact, if you give them a pendulum to experiment with, they'll make sure it won't move by holding their arms rigidly while at the same time failing to concentrate on making it move. The best way to handle people like this is to refuse to engage. It's a waste of time to try to discuss the subject with those determined to prove you wrong. Smile, remain pleasant no matter what they might say, and suggest they read a book on the subject. If they become interested in the subject after reading, say that you'd be happy to help them.

Keep positive as you continue your practice, and remember even experienced dowsers get inaccurate results every now and then. Fortunately your success rate will increase over time and with practice, so long as you are consistent with it. And as your expertise with the pendulum grows, your intuitive skills will also develop. Your pendulum enables you to reach well beyond the five usual senses and communicate with the Divine.

The pendulum has enhanced my life in many ways, and I'm sure it will do the same for you. I wish you great success with it.

# Bibliography

Bell, A. H., ed. *Practical Dowsing: A Symposium*. G. Bell & Sons, 1965.

Bird, Christopher. *The Divining Hand: The 500-Year-Old Mystery of Dowsing*. E. P. Dutton, 1979.

Friedman, Isidore. *The Mathematics of Consciousness*. The Society for the Study of the Natural Order, 1974.

Jacobsen, Annie. *Phenomena: The Secret History of the U.S. Government's Investigation into Extrasensory Perception and Psychokinesis*. Little, Brown and Company, 2017.

Steiger, Brad. *ESP: Your Sixth Sense*. Award Books, 1966.

Webster, Richard. *How to Use a Pendulum: 50 Practical Rituals and Spiritual Activities*. Llewellyn Publications, 2020.

Webster, Richard. *Pendulum Magic for Beginners*. Llewellyn Publications, 2002.

Wilson, Colin. *Beyond the Occult: The Astonishing Conclusion to the Occult Trilogy*. Bantam Press, 1988.

# To Write to the Author

If you wish to contact the author or would like more information about this book, please write to the author in care of Llewellyn Worldwide and we will forward your request. Both the author and the publisher appreciate hearing from you and learning of your enjoyment of this book and how it has helped you. Llewellyn Worldwide cannot guarantee that every letter written to the author can be answered, but all will be forwarded.

Please write to:

Richard Webster
℅ Llewellyn Worldwide
2143 Wooddale Drive
Woodbury, MN 55125-2989

Please enclose a self-addressed stamped envelope for reply or $1.00 to cover costs. If outside the USA, enclose an international postal reply coupon.

Many of Llewellyn's authors have websites with additional information and resources. For more information, please visit our website at https://www.llewellyn.com

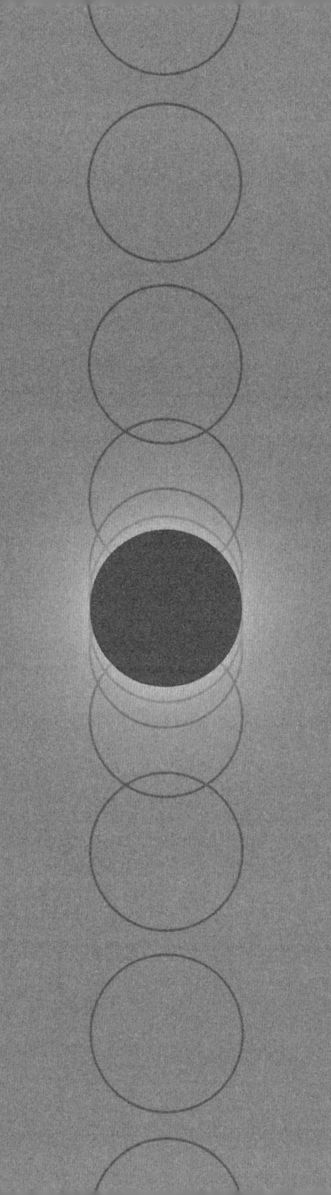